ISH I
Thus

CW01468619

Autobiography of Joseph Priestley

PRIESTLEY
JOSEPH LL.D. F.R.S.

Autobiography of Joseph Priestley

Introduction by Jack Lindsay

Memoirs written by Himself

An Account of Further Discoveries in Air

Adams & Dart, Bath

© 1970, Adams & Dart
First published in 1970 by
Adams & Dart, 40 Gay Street, Bath, Somerset
All rights reserved

SBN 239.00047.1

Printed in Great Britain by Billing & Sons Ltd
Guildford and London

Preface

There has been only one substantial reprint of Priestley's Memoirs: that by John Towill Rutt, who used it as the basis of his Life and Correspondence of Joseph Priestley in two volumes, 1832. But he breaks into it with very many letters and voluminous notes, often distracting rather than helpful, so that it is not easy to read it as a narrative in itself; and he makes several cuts. Dr. Robert E. Schofield in A Scientific Autobiography of Joseph Priestley, 1966, cites only the passages connected with Priestley's scientific development. The present issue is, then, the sole direct and complete reprint of the Memoirs of 1806. I have inserted also what amounts to a Journal by Priestley of his tour in France, and one of his most important pamphlets, An Account of Further Discoveries in Air, has been reprinted in full after the Memoirs. Footnotes in the Memoirs were added by Priestley's son.

I have added an Introduction, which provides some further biographical facts and details of Priestley's scientific work, to supplement the Memoirs, and then attempts to assess his relation to Hartley and to Boscovich, and the reasons for his refusing to accept Lavoisier's formulations. Dr. Schofield has done important work in the analysis of his scientific thinking; and L. L. Whyte's book on Boscovich, with his own essay and those of his contributors, supplies an essential part of the background. However, I have felt that it was worthwhile to make use of these researches within a wider focus, in which I trust that I have managed to bring out more fully than has been done the vital unity of Priestley's many interests and branches of work, social, political philosophical, theological, and scientific (whether concerned with electricity, optics, chemistry). I feel that when this inter-linkage of all his ideas and positions is realised, his stature grows considerably; and many of the notions born of a superficial or limited analysis of his ideas need to be corrected and amplified.

JACK LINDSAY

Contents

Introduction

1 *Joseph Priestley*

Yorkshire in the eighteenth century was a busy and earnest place. Dissent throve among the craftsmen who, though drawn into the growing manu- factory system, often combined farming and textile work. Joseph Priestley came from the heart of this independent and hard-working class. His grandfather, of the same name, was settled at one of the white-cloth centres, Birstal Fieldhead, near Leeds. A maker and dresser of cloth, in good times he perhaps employed some ten men in the workshops by his house. He was brought up in the Church of England; but his strong- minded wife, Sarah Healey (Hayley), imposed Calvinism on the family while bearing eight children. Of the sons John and Jonas stayed on at Birstal, while two of the girls married well-off men at Heckmondwike nearby. Jonas worked as a dresser, but in a smaller way than his father, and married Mary, daughter of Joseph Swift, farmer and maltster near Shafton. Four children had been borne when she died in the winter of the Great Frost (1739–40), in childbed.[1]

Joseph, her eldest, was born at the corner of Owler Lane in 1733 on 13 March (24 March, new style); on 19 June next year his brother Timothy was born, who became a Calvinist minister under the patronage of Selina Countess of Huntingdon; a third brother, Joshua, became a clothmaker at Leeds. Of the two girls, Mary died at three; but Martha lived on to admire her eldest brother. When a few weeks old, Joseph was put in a basket and taken with his mother on horseback to be shown to his grand- father Swift. When he was about four, he went to stay at Shafton (some four miles past Wakefield) until after his mother's death. Then his brothers took his place at Shafton, and he, at home, attended a nearby school. His father, struggling to cope with his large family, married a widow, formerly Hannah Holdsworth of Wakefield, who had been housekeeper to Dr. Philip Doddridge, the minister who taught at a Northampton academy. Hannah bore Jonas three girls.

When nine, Joseph went to live at Old Hall, Heckmondwike, with his father's elder sister Sarah who, childless, had been married seventeen years to John Keighley. Keighley died within three years; but the boy remained with his aunt till her death in 1764. He went to various local schools, then, when about eleven, to a free school, probably Batley Grammar School (where Joseph Hague was usher, 1744–6). Falling badly ill, apparently of tuberculosis of the lungs, he was tenderly nursed by his aunt. Later Timothy, in a funeral sermon that mingles family pride and a conviction of Joseph's damnation, stated that about this time came the first signs of scientific interest:

My brother began to discover a taste for experiments when about eleven years of age. The first he made was on spiders, and by putting them into bottles, he found how long they could live without fresh air. The second was the power of the leaver, and I well remember how much these experiments pleased him. He soon told me how many men he could lift from the ground in a moment, &c. &c.

My brother, when he began to learn astronomy, would be in the fields with his pen and papers; this spread his fame, as it was at that time a science very little known. When he found out any thing new, I was soon acquainted with it: I remember when he was making much progress in electricity, in showing me how to melt steel; when the metal melted, he called, Oh had Sir Isaac Newton seen such an experiment! and his pleasure on those occasions cannot well be described.[2]

Joseph himself says that he had not experimented in any original way before 1765. By thirteen he had read most of Bunyan as well as other religious works together with the Latin school authors. He trained himself in composition by writing out sermons that he heard; his fluency increased after he learned shorthand. His aunt wanted to see him a minister. After two years he left the grammar school; by sixteen, advanced in his study of languages, he was allowed to work on his own. Probably about 1750–2 he began to be interested in a general way in science. But the state of his health made his aunt think he had better turn to commerce than to the ministry; he took up modern languages and was sent to a merchant uncle. But at the last moment, feeling his health improved, he decided that he would prefer the ministry or medicine. So in 1752, aged nineteen, he went to a new academy at Daventry under Dr. Caleb Ashworth, where he was the first pupil enrolled. The Northampton academy had ended with Dr. Doddridge's death the previous October; and the only alternative was an academy in London (at Plasterer's Hall, then at Mile End after 1754) which was strictly Calvinist. Joseph was breaking away from his family's tenets, which continued to hold Timothy. However, before he left for Daventry he was introduced to mathematics by a man trained under Colin Maclaurin, friend and disciple of Newton, at Edinburgh; and when he did arrive, he was far more advanced than most of the other students.

He had studied W. S. J. v. 'sGravesande's work, no doubt the version made from the Latin as *Mathematical Elements of Natural Philosophy Confirmed by Experiment, or an Introduction to Sir Isaac Newton's Philosophy*, which encouraged experiments aimed at establishing the principles of astronomy and elementary mechanics. He seems to have followed out the courses there suggested; and Timothy's memories of levers and astronomy would belong to this period.[3] Dr. Isaac Watts, the hymn-writer, had written a catechism and textbooks much used by Dissenters, who felt strengthened by his championship of civil and religious liberty. Watts' thought had influenced Doddridge, whose academy examined controversial matters from all sides; and it now affected the system at Daventry. Daventry certainly carried on Doddridge's curriculum of 'lectures on the Principles of *Geometry* and *Algebra*', with

the knowledge of *Trigonometry, Conic-sections* and *celestial Mechanics* (A Collection of important Propositions, taken chiefly from Sir Isaac Newton, and demonstrated, independent on the rest. They relate especially, tho' not only, to centripetal and centrifugal Forces). A system of natural and experimental Philosophy, comprehending *Mechanics, Statics, Hydrostatics, Optics, Pneumatics,* and *Astronomy,* was read.[4]

The system 'was illustrated by a neat and pretty large *philosophical Apparatus*' and 'a distinct view of the Anatomy of the human Body was given'. In 1781 we find much the same curriculum being used, plus 'the new discoveries upon Air' and an enlarged apparatus, now covering also 'Electricity and the Airs', though somewhat deficient 'in the Optical and Astronomical departments'.[5]

At Daventry Priestley also read Hartley, whose psychology was meant to provide a justification of the theological Doctrine of Necessity. He absorbed the enthusiastic sense of Necessity (the rule of mechanical law) operating in the human sphere as well as the natural and somehow proving the possibility of 'human perfectibility'. These years were, then, decisive for his development. At Daventry he took in all the most advanced positions of the Dissenters and prepared himself for his work in which scientific, religious, social, and psychological elements were all drawn into a single focus. The Dissenters, shut out of the ruling system and disqualified for all public preferment, were unable to graduate at Oxford or Cambridge; in return they created academies far more alive and linked with the needs of the time than the bodies from which they were excluded. The tradition of the Independents from which Priestley came went back to Cromwellian days, though it had adapted itself to the situation emerging after the so-called Revolution of 1688–9 and now expressed the outlook of men leading the way into a new world of economic and social action.

Priestley read Boerhaave's *Elementa Chemiae,* dealt with at least ten folio pages of Greek daily (together with Alexander of Birmingham, who became a fine Greek scholar and critic of the Bible); he began to write down his conclusions. In 1755 he drafted *Institutes of Natural and Revealed Religion* (printed in revised form some seventeen years later). He also studied afresh Newton, with Locke and Stahl.

In 1755 he left to be assistant minister to a congregation at Needham Market, Suffolk, where he soon created troubles for himself. He refused help from bodies whose views he could not accept; he gave lectures on the Institutes or theory of religion as a 'furious freethinker' (his own phrase later). With reduced salary, he made known that he was starting a school; but no pupils came. His aunt stopped her allowance. Only the aid of well-wishers with funds to help ministers in their first difficult days kept him going. His inherited stammer grew worse. But his relenting aunt helped him to take a course of treatment; and at least as a byproduct of his setbacks he had time to study and paid some visits to Cambridge. He corresponded with Hartley on the application of his ideas to education, and was offered aid if he wanted to publish his findings. However, Hartley died in 1757.

He preached a trial sermon at Sheffield, but was not approved. Still, a minister there, Haynes, recommended him to his former congregation at Nantwich in Cheshire. Priestley moved in 1758. Now he was again in a manufacturing region, salt being the main product. His flock was made up in part of travelling packmen, often Scots, and he found that his doctrines did not rouse such antagonism. He opened a school and soon had some thirty boys and six girls, teaching from 7 a.m. to 4 p.m. with an hour's dinner break. After school he acted as tutor to the family of a rich attorney; and found time to play the flute. He grew interested in livelier ways of teaching history.

He stayed on till September 1761 when he was asked to act as tutor in languages and belles-lettres at Warrington Academy, where John Holt was tutor in mathematics and natural philosophy. The letter recommending Priestley to the trustees mentioned his 'unexceptionable character', his 'steady attachment to the Principles of Civil and Religious Liberty', and the degree of 'Critical & Classical Learning not common in one so young'. And in 1761 he was praised for his ability in languages and his 'singular genius for the management of youth'. He was not yet known as a scientist,[6]

In 1762 his *Theory of Language, and Universal Grammar* was published as an outline, to be filled out by the tutor. One point he often made was that the language had been 'fixed' only recently, under Queen Anne, so that there was a chance of preserving it 'to the latest ages' through its

very simplicity. He mentioned three courses of History he had worked
out. In these he stressed the interaction of the sciences and the arts that
was going on; society was bringing improvement to the useful arts and
the arts were favouring 'society and humanity', which again in turn
stimulated all the sciences. We find him using charts and models in his
lectures, and showing how early events could be dated by reference to
eclipses. Friendly with many students, he took part in the production of
plays. Mrs. Barbauld later remembered how 'dancing, cards, the theatres,
were all held lawful in moderation'.[7]

A good account of his work as teacher has been left by one of his pupils,
Simpson:

What Dr. Priestley added in discoursing from his written lectures (most of
which are since published to the world) was pointedly and clearly illustrative
of the subject before him, and expressed with great simplicity and distinct-
ness of language, though he sometimes manifested that difficulty of utterance
which he mentions in the Memoirs of his life. At the conclusion of his
lecture he always encouraged the students to express their sentiments
relative to the subjects of it, and to urge any objection to what he had
delivered without reserve. It pleased him when any one commenced such a
conversation. In order to excite the freest discussion, he occasionally invited
the students to drink tea with him, in order to canvas the subjects of his
lectures. I do not recollect that he ever shewed the least displeasure at the
strongest objections that were made to what he delivered; but distinctly
remember the smile of approbation with which he usually received them
nor did he fail to point out in a very encouraging manner the ingenuity or
force of any remarks that were made, when they merited these characters.
His object, as well as Dr. Aikin's, was to engage the students to examine
and decide for themselves, uninfluenced by the sentiments of any other
person. His written lectures he used to permit each student to take and
read in his own lodgings. Those on Rhetoric he gave them the liberty of
copying, those on History of reading only, as he intended them for publication. From minutes in short-hand, he dictated to each student, by turns, one
of the lectures on History, who copied after him in long-hand. From this
copy the Doctor told me they were printed, with some additions only,
relative to subsequent events.

A new building for the academy was nearing its end; and while Seddon
was seeking financial aid in London, Priestley took over his role as minister
at Warrington. He also tried to arrange a chemistry lecture, which seems
not to have come off. In May he was preparing for ordination, as he meant
to get married.

I can sincerely say, I never knew what it was to be anxious on my own
account; but I cannot help confessing I begin to feel a good deal on the
account of another person. The hazard of bringing a person into difficulties

which she⁻cannot probably have any idea or prospect of, affects me at times very sensibly.[8]

When the new building was finished, Priestley as one of the tutors could claim a house, though he would have to put up some students there as well. At Wrexham on 23 June 1762 he married Mary Wilkinson, whose brothers were to become important iron-masters; she herself was a capable strong character, well-suited to be Priestley's wife. He now was visiting Liverpool, where at Thomas Bentley's house he met many interesting persons, including Josiah Wedgwood. Bentley, who had founded a public library at Liverpool in 1758, represented the Corporation in all important matters in London and before Parliament – though he was strongly opposed to the slave trade on which much of the town's wealth depended. The surgeon Matthew Turner was a friend of Bentley and Priestley drew him in as a lecturer on chemistry. Turner is said to have made the first commercial preparation of sulphuric ether [diethyl ether], and he supplied Josiah Wedgwood and Matthew Boulton with varnishes, lacquers, and metallic powders. He it was who drew Wedgwood from empirical procedures to scientific method. An atheist, he later replied as 'Hammon' to Priestley's *Letters to a Philosophical Unbeliever* (1780). There he complimented Priestley as a man who might have gone far in science if he had not been dedicated to religion; and it is of interest that already in 1762 he expressed a high opinion of him in a letter to Seddon. In *Philosophical Empiricism* (1775) Priestley recalled how:

when I attended a course of chemical lectures, delivered at Warrington, by the ingenious Mr. Turner of Liverpool, I was one who assisted in the making of a quantity of Spirit of nitre [nitric acid], in a manner not so expeditious, indeed, as that which I suppose is now generally used, but in which I am pretty confident there was no opportunity for any common air to get into the composition of.[9]

For the course Turner was no doubt drawing on William Lewis's *Commercium Philosophico-Technicum or the Philosophical Commerce of Arts* (1763–5), which was in the Warrington Library, as part of the academy's keen efforts to link knowledge and craft.[10] Warrington itself was a busy centre of manufacture and trade: sail-cloth made of hemp and flax imported from Russia via Liverpool, pins, locks, hinges. A certain amount of copper-smelting, glass-making, sugar-refining, foundry-work, brewing and malting went on, and there were many inns for the large number of passers-through.

Turner's lectures in 1763-5, 'a full course of practical and commercial Chemistry', may well have done much to stir Priestley's interest in experiments. It was, however, to problems of electricity that he first turned. For the moment he was absorbed in compiling a Biographical Chart, which was drawn to the attention of the academy's president, who in turn suggested application to Birch, the Royal Society's secretary, in the event of difficulties. In July 1764 Priestley wrote to Birch about the dates of a Tatar prince and an Arabian poet. The Chart, published, was a great success. His friends managed to get the degree of Doctor of Laws conferred on him by the University of Edinburgh for his educational work on 4 December 1764. He had been composing an *Essay on a course of liberal education for civil and active life,* a defence of his system with its combination of the religious, the philosophic (intellectual and scientific), and the utilitarian. He declared that one of the great needs of the time was a history of experimental philosophy; and he made up his mind to start such a work by grappling first with electricity. Seddon, at his request, gave him a letter of introduction to John Canton, who had started as apprentice to a cloth weaver and became a headmaster, writing scientific journalism—and now become a member of the Royal Society's Council. He had been the first Englishman to confirm Franklin's hypothesis of the electrical nature of lightning; and Priestley was turning to him as a leading theorist on electricity. On 18 December 1765 Priestley climbed into the coach for London, embarking on his scientific career. Through Canton he soon had met several important scientific figures and attended his first meeting of the Royal Society on 9 January 1766. Among his new acquaintances were Franklin, William Watson, and Richard Price. On 12 June 1766 he was elected a Fellow of the Royal Society.

In 1767 appeared *The History and Present State of Electricity, with Original Experiments,* followed soon by *A Familiar Introduction to the Study of Electricity* and his first paper in *The Philosophical Transactions of the Royal Society,* 'An account of Rings consisting of all the Prismatic Colours, made by Electrical Explosions in the Surface of Pieces of Metal' – read in March 1768. The next year saw the second editions of the two books and two more papers on the Force of Electrical Explosions.[11] In *The History* he has fully developed his method of exposition, describing all the stages and details of an experiment, with any mistakes or setbacks. His mind ranged over many possibilities in the electrical field, even if he did not follow them up. He was interested in the connection of electricity with chemistry, both sciences dealing with the latent or less obvious properties of bodies; light, he thought, would prove the key to electrical phenomena and other yet unknown properties of bodies; he was pondering the old problem of the likeness between calcination of metals and respiration processes in animal or plant; he drew attention to the importance of knowledge about 'the Atmosphere, its composition and affections'. He already considered that a combination of electricity, chemistry and optics would provide a valuable basis for grappling with the question of the nature of matter. Thus, in dealing with any particular phenomenon, he was thinking all the time of ways towards a comprehensive scientific grasp and wanted to cover all the fields of hidden forces and material changes, while adding the mathematics of vision and light. Franklin, Canton, Watson provided him with much material and read his work critically as it advanced, while in Price he found a man close to his own breadth of outlook, an expert on actuarial mathematics who was also a theologian and radical politician. For some thirty years scientific amateurs had been playing about with electricity, but Priestley was soon making discoveries of his own, much interested in conductivity and comparative resistances; he set out the force law between electrical charges and discovered the so-called electrical wind. Like Aepinus, a little before him, he realised that the distinction between conductors and insulators was far from absolute; he used the length of a spark-gap to measure the circuit's resistance. And, repeating Franklin's experiment to prove the absence of charge in an electrified hollow vessel of metal, he deduced the theorem that the attraction of electricity varied proportionately to the inverse square of the distance. He thus provided a prediction to which verification could be applied. Two years later, (1769), Robison verified it, and then Cavendish, designing one of his ingenious apparatus by which a metal sphere might be enclosed in another, with or without electrical contact between them; he found that the applied charge was always confined to the outer sphere. As for Priestley, he inevitably at times missed points in his experiments or failed to grasp some of the variables present. A letter of 1767, like his second paper of 1769, dealt with 'the momentum of electrical matter in explosions', and in the letter [to Canton] he went so far as to conjecture that 'there is no electric fluid at all, and that electrification is only some modification of the matter of which any body consisted before that operation'.[12]

A passage in his 1767 book brings out the exalted mood with which he tackled the problems of science, the breadth of his vision from the outset, and the way in which he was concerned essentially throughout his career with the nature of matter and its changes rather than with some incidental branch of research:

Hitherto philosophy has been chiefly conversant about the more sensible properties of bodies; electricity, together with chymistry, and the doctrine of light and colours, seems to be giving us an inlet into their internal structure, on which their sensible properties depend. By pursuing this new light therefore, the bounds of natural science may possibly be extended, beyond what we can now form an idea of. New worlds may open to our view, and the glory of the great Sir Isaac Newton himself, and all his contemporaries be eclisped [*sic*], by a new set of philosophers, in a quite new field of speculation.[13]

Note there the key-phrase *an inlet into their internal structure.* We shall see as we go on how original Priestley was in such a concept, and the debt he owed to Boscovich in this connection.

The academy continued to meet with difficulties, and Mrs. Priestley felt that the banks of the river Mersey did not suit her constitution. Priestley had been preaching in a number of places, and in September 1769 the family (now with a daughter Sally) moved to Leeds. There he was minister at Mill-Hill Chapel for six years, during which time two sons were borne by Mary. As always, his interests and activities continued to be widely extended, but his main scientific interest shifted to Optics, while in the religious field he became a Socinian and started on the series of theological works that made him the main spokesman for Unitarianism in England. In his *Institutes of Natural and Revealed Religion* he discarded a great deal of what was considered Christianity as 'idolatrous', urged the use of reason, and declared, 'Have nothing to with a parliamentary religion, or a parliamentary God'. During his Leeds' years he published 28 non-scientific works in first editions, 10 in second, and three each in third and fourth editions; four new books on science, two in revised editions, and a volume of Additions to one of them; he also had seven papers in the Transactions. And all the while he was corresponding with persons from all over Europe on educationl and scientific matters. He tried to carry on with his plans for his comprehensive history of the sciences, published a book on the theory and practice of perspective and another, *The History and Present State of Discoveries relating to Vision, Light and Colours,* in 1772. In this he included no original work, and the book was not a success, most of the subscribers to the 500 copies defaulting in payment. Depressed, he dropped his plans for the series; if he was to work for nothing, he told Canton, he preferred to stick to theology.

Indeed, though he truly claimed that he never based his work or career on any aim of self-advancement, he was feeling the pinch. His family expenses were increasing, and he considered the making and selling of scientific apparatus. Timothy says, 'Many electrifying machines were made, and sold to friends'. He adds:

When we had each a small family, finding I could work in either brass or wood, and turn his work on a lathe, though I had never been taught, he proposed a partnership, for making electrifying machines; for though he had such natural abilities, he could scarcely handle any tool. Then having a child added to my number almost every year, and but £60 *per ann.* he wished to help me, more than himself.[14]

Joseph himself was collecting scientific books and apparatus; at the time of the Birmingham riots his set of 'philosophical instruments' was one of the best in the world. Now, in his difficulties, he was attracted by an invitation to go with Banks as astronomer on Cook's second voyage, with the offer of 'handsome provision' for himself and his family. It is hard to see why he was chosen for the job, though most of the work would consist of comparing techniques in measuring longitude; but in any event the fact, or the threat, of clerical opposition put a stop to the project. The same opposition obstructed his inquiries into the possibilities of emigrating to America.

From 1770 his electrical studies had given way to chemistry, with a transitional paper on experiments with charcoal. He here showed his adherence to the Phlogiston school, remarking on the 'completeness of the union that is produced between the inflammable principle and its base'. He seems to have been much better read in chemical literature by this time than the *Memoirs* suggests. In 1772 he issued a pamphlet on his invention of artificially carbonated water; and this led on to his award of the Copley Medal in 1773 for a paper on 'different Kinds of Air'. Once again it is hard to make out the precise reason for a jump in his interests: this time to 'fixed air' (carbon dioxide) and its uses in an antiscorbutic. But he may have had his mind drawn to the theme by some comments in the *Monthly Review* (1767) where W. Bewley was dealing with his *History of Electricity*. His letters reveal his growing mastery of chemical experiment, from uncertainties in 1767–8 into work on meliorating plants (1771), and then on to work on nitrous air (nitric oxide) and its uses in eudiometry as well as on acid air (anhydrous hydrochloric acid). He discovered photosynthesis, the absorption of carbon dioxide by green plants in sunlight with production of oxygen, independently of IngenHousz. On 24 November 1787 he wrote to the latter in terms that reveal his fine lack of vanity and generosity of spirit. He had received a work by IngenHousz:

I am sorry to perceive, in the preface, something that looks as if you, or your friends, thought I wished to detract from your merit, which is very far from being my disposition. . . . That plants restore vitiated air, I discovered at a very early period. Afterwards I found that the air in which they are confined was sometimes better than common air, and that the green matter, which I at first, and several of my friends always, thought to be a vegetable produced pure air by means of light. Immediately after the publication of these facts, and before I had seen your book, I had found that other whole plants did the same. All the time that I was making these experiments, I wrote to my friends about them, particularly to Mr. Magellan, and desired him to communicate my observations to you, as well as to others; but I believe you had not heard of them; so that what you did with *leaves* was altogether independent of what I was doing with *whole plants*. The same summer, and the same sun, operated for us both, and you certainly published before me.

This appears to me to be a true state of the case; and surely it leaves no room for suspicion of anything unfair, or unfriendly. But whatever your friends may say, I have no thought of troubling the public with any vindication. I value you, and your friendship, too much to wish to have any altercation on the subject. Indeed, there is nothing to contend about. If, on any future occasion, you will do me the justice to give this state of the matter, I shall be happy. If not, I shall not complain.[15]

This modesty was characteristic of Priestley in all his relationships. Thus, on 20 February 1780 he had written to the Rev. W. Ashdowne of Dover (where he carried on a considerable manufactory) about a tract:

You and I have the same idea concerning supernatural influence, and of the bad use that has been made of the popular doctrine on that subject; but you have taken much more pains, and have been much more successful in the investigation of the sense of scripture.[16]

Within five years of starting work on gases Priestley had further made:

(1) those early observations on gaseous diffusion which, with his later experiments on the same subject, were to influence Dalton's studies; (2) the beginning observations on flame and electric-spark colours in different gases, so suggestive of spectral phenomena; (3) the gas-density observations, which he ignored, to his subsequent confusion, as he characteristically did gravimetric data; and (4) his volumetric observations on the diminution of common and nitrous airs over iron and brimstone – these last two demonstrating his capacity for quantitative experimentation if he wished. [SCHOFIELD][17]

Also, we can see from his letters and his paper that he had already (by 1771) prepared oxygen by heating nitre. He noted the fact and its 'very extraordinary and important' nature, which, 'in able hands, may lead to considerable discoveries'. Later, on 1 August 1774, he got the gas by concentrating solar rays on red calx of mercury (*mercurius calcinatus per se*) through a powerful converging lens. Clearly chemical studies were ripe for the discovery, which was made independently by Robison and Scheele.

In all this work he was assuming the existence of phlogiston, the inflammable principle or food-of-fire, a substance emitted during combustion and the calcination of metals. The total or almost total combustion of bodies like sulphur, charcoal, phosphorus, was taken to prove them to be very rich in phlogiston; and the formation of acids (sulphuric, phosphoric, etc.) from the solution of the fumes showed them to be composed of the acid plus phlogiston. When metal was heated, the phlogiston was driven out and left a calx: so calx plus phlogiston made up the metal. When the calx was heated with charcoal, phlogiston was exchanged and the metal restored. The phlogiston theory brought together and made intelligible a wide series of reactions.

The summer of 1773 saw a large-scale change in Priestley's circumstances. Price had hinted to William Petty, second Earl of Shelburne, that Priestley needed a patron; and Shelburne, who admired Priestley, tactfully approached him with the offer of the post of librarian. (The Earl was descended on the female side from Sir William Petty, the financier and scientist of the seventeenth century; as a member of Chatham's cabinet he opposed the King's policy over the American Colonies and was dismissed in 1768. Now, out of office, he was fighting against the measures taken by Lord North.) After some hesitation Priestley accepted the offer, which increased his earnings two-and-a-half times. On 16 May he preached his farewell sermon, remarking on the extent to which at Leeds 'I have been at full liberty to speak, write, or do, whatever I have judged' to be in the general interests of Christianity. 'I do not know many congregations of dissenters in England, so numerous as that of Leeds, where I could have been so happy in this respect.'

At Calne, the Earl's country estate, the Priestleys lived as his friends rather than his employees. In autumn 1774 Priestley went with Shelburne on a tour of the Continent. Despite all the great differences he was able to make himself at home in the Paris of the Encyclopaedists. Once when he was dining with Turgot, M. de Chastellux remarked that

the two gentlemen opposite me were the Bishop of Aix and the Archbishop of Toulouse, 'but', said he, 'they are no more believers than you or I'. I assured him that he was a believer; but he would not believe me, and le Roi, the philosopher, told me that I was the only man of sense he knew that was a Christian.[18]

At another dinner party, where Lavoisier was present, Priestley told the company of his discovery of 'a kind of air in which the candle burnt much better than in common air'. Lavoisier saw in this remark a clue to his own experimental results, and followed up with more experiments on the combustion of substances such as sulphur, phosphorus, and carbonaceous materials; he was thus led to his theory of acids. By 1783 he had definitely given up phlogiston and introduced his *principe oxygine*.

During the seven years Priestley spent with Shelburne he spent the summer at Calne, then wintered in the Earl's London house. His work was to catalogue the books and papers, and to direct the education of the two sons (there was also a tutor). The Earl was pleased to learn through him the views of the dissenting Whigs. There was a fair amount of lesiure for chemical work; and he now isolated and identified ammonia, sulphur dioxide, oxygen, nitrous oxide, and nitrogen dioxide – or to use his terms, alkaline air, vitriolic acid air, dephlogisticated air, dephlogisticated nitrous air, and nitrous acid air.[19] He also composed important general works such as *Disquisitions Relating to Matter and Spirit*, 1777. His high reputation is shown by such facts as his inclusion in the invitation made by Cavendish on 27 May 1775 to five persons to witness his experiments with an artificial torpedo: the others were Hunter the anatomist, Lane the inventor of the discharging electrometer, Nairne the scientific instrument-maker, and Ronayne, who was said to be sceptical as to the electrical nature of the genus *torpedo* itself.[20]

As a preparation for his *Disquisitions* he republished in 1775 Hartley's *Theory of the Human Mind* and went on gathering observations on human nature to illustrate the *Theory*. In time he compiled several volumes of them, which were destroyed in the 1791 riots. His *Disquisitions* brought together Newton's mechanism, Hartley's psychology, and Boscovich's atomism. Boscovich, a Jesuit, was outraged, and complained bitterly to Shelburne. On 19 August Priestley replied:

I am very sorry to have any cause of complaint against a person for whom I have always had so great an esteem as I have had for the Abbé Boscovich— You have been informed, it seems that I have represented you as 'a favourer of the most extravagant' materialism: which you consider as 'abominable, detestable, and impious'. You call my conduct 'an atrocious calumny, which attacks your religion, probity, and honour'. You say, I 'must retract what I have advanced, that I shall find in you a zealous opponent, that you shall be obliged to give public notice, in the Journals, of this insult of mine upon you, and that what I have advanced has been without even reading your book'.
All this, and more to the same purpose, you express in a letter to Lord Shelburne, which his Lordship has just put into my hands. Now I cannot

help observing that, had you had something better than mere *hearsay* for all this, it would have become a man of honour to have remonstrated to *myself* on the subject, and not to have immediately written to my patron about it; when you must have been sensible, that it could only tend to do me an injury; and for any thing that you knew, it might have been an irreparable and fatal one. . . .
Whatever guilt I have contracted by my late publication, I have not made *you* an accomplice with me in it; for that I have only adopted your theory of *the nature of the matter*, without supposing that you had the most distant idea of the *use* that I have made of it . . .
You must allow me to say that, after the many very agreeable conversations that I had with you at Paris, in which I frequently expressed a high approbation of your work, I am particularly surprised that you could suppose I had quoted it without having read it myself.[21]

Priestley was very hurt, but did not make things better by adding remarks about 'the church of Rome, of which you are a member; but which I consider as properly *antichristian*, and a system of abominations little better than heathenism'. Boscovich, who did not understand English, wrote back on 17 October, from near Sens, in milder terms, but holding to his main point and insisting that the book 'must do me infinite injury among the large numbers of persons who do not examine things thoroughly and who know your great reputation in natural philosophy [*Physique*]'. He was no doubt already suffering from the melancholia that killed him in 1787, and had his own good reasons for fearing the troubles he might meet through too close a connection with a materialism such as Priestley's.[22]

Disquisitions indeed caused wide offence and must have played its part in the ending of Priestley's position at Calne. Shelburne's own views were those of Price rather than of Priestley; in December 1786 he told Price that if Priestley resolved to form a sect he could only call them 'atheistical Christians, men who would not believe in a God if it was not for Jesus Christ'. But a man like Priestley could indeed not feel quite at home in a nobleman's house, however liberal the treatment; and Shelburne had married a year before the break, which meant changes in the household. The new Lady Shelburne is said to have brought about the break. Further, Priestley had been ill; suffering in the 1780 summer from what seems his first attack of gallstones.

That he should turn now to Birmingham was natural enough. His work had gained him more and more links with the advanced thinkers there. By 1780 he knew Boulton, James Keir, William Withering, and the Rev. Radcliffe Scholefield, minister of the main dissenting meeting-house. In September 1780, with a pension from Shelburne, he moved to Fair Hill, near the Sparkbrook turnpike-gate, with the help of his brother-in-law,

John Wilkinson. He became one of the two ministers of the New Meeting-house and was able to meet and discuss things with the members of the Lunar Society, that brilliant group of thinkers who played such an important part in facilitating the new industrial developments, and who were regarded as bumptious upstarts by the sterile intellectuals of the ruling class. 'It has often struck us,' said a reviewer of Priestley's *Memoirs* in 1806, 'that there is universally something presumptious in provincial genius.' Boulton was the rock on which the new edifice was built. The Society was foreshadowed when he and Erasmus Darwin grew friendly; John Whitehurst, the Derby clockmaker, was another early recruit, with Josiah Wedgwood as a stalwart member. Others were Thomas Day, R. L. Edgeworth, the younger Samuel Galton, James Watt, Keir. The reaction that set in against the French Revolution broke up the group and by the end of the century it was dissolved. Keir may be taken as an example of these men. An able chemist, he wrote also on geology, politics, and military strategy; managed a glass-works, directed manufactures at Soho for Boulton, and finally ran a chemical works at Tipton.

Despite the stimulus of the Lunar Society, Priestley's scientific work did not progress. He published two volumes of experiments, but the first was mainly made up of work done at Calne; and in the second volume about a quarter was taken up with reprints of papers of 1783–5. The new papers did not break fresh ground. He was throwing himself with renewed vigour into the polemical field of theology, where his positions were strongly linked with the social and political views of himself and his more advanced colleagues. His *History of the Corruptions of Christianity*, 1782, stirred up much wrath and denunciation; as a result he began a yearly volume of *Defences of Unitarianism*. He also published a four-volume *History of Early Opinions Concerning Jesus Christ*, in 1786, and the first two volumes of a *General History of the Christian Church*, 1790. There were more than a dozen volumes of this sort of studies, plus many pamphlets and printed sermons; he was also doing editorial work on the revived *Theological Repository* (1784, 1786, 1788). No doubt his increased sense of freedom and his closer contacts with radical dissenting groups helped to turn him to the controversial religious field; also he may well have felt a worsening of strain in the political field, as, following the protracted American conflict, the French situation moved towards revolution. When that revolution emerged, he felt the need to defend the new developments and set up a stronger resistance to reaction; he set out his views in three pamphlets (1787, 1790, 1791). In his correspondence he mingled his interests in science and theology. Thus on 28 August 1775 he wrote to the Rev. N. Cappe of York:

I have made many observations on human nature, with a view to the illustration of Hartley's theory. They relate very much to the conduct of the mind and happiness, and they are so necessarily intermixed with observations on education, that I almost think it will be best to publish them altogether as one work, and consequently not very soon. . . . I am satisfied that my argument for Peter not being one of the two disciples going to Emmaus was not well founded. I think to print the Greek Harmony this winter, and the English some time after. . . . Among other things, I have a new interpretation of Daniel's prophecy of seventy weeks.

The sparry acid is an acid contained in what the chymists call *fluor*. In Derbyshire it is called *spar*, and they make vases and ornaments for chimney-pieces of it. The acid air is procured by pouring upon it oil of vitriol, and receiving the produce in quicksilver, as with the marine acid air. The first section in my new volume is on the vitriolic acid air, which is procured by heating on it anything containing phlogiston. . . . I should think myself happy if I had an opportunity of shewing your son some of my late experiments. I do not wonder at your anxiety about him, and shall rejoice when a suitable employment is provided for him.[23]

On 9 June 1786 he wrote to Martin von Marum, secretary of the Society of Science in Haarlem, who was well known for his work with a large static electrical machine:

I shall be happy to receive the second part of your experiments, with the great electrical machine, not doubting but they will give me as much pleasure as the first has done. I ordered my bookseller to send you the 6th volume of experiments just published, and likewise my *History of early Opinions concerning Christ* 4 vols I hope you will soon receive them, and I shall be glad to find that they give you any satisfaction.[24]

Clearly he felt there was no dividing line between Hartleian materialism, a rational socially-conscious religion, and scientific research into the laws of nature. Regenerating systems of education and even the stabilising of the character of a difficult son flowed logically from the materialism and the experiments. The vital unity of all Priestley's ideas and actions, at all stages of his life, is what gives him his force and his interest. His work was now reaching a wider audience. In 1787 Joseph Gales, a Gateshead printer, launched his *Register* and started a new style in provincial journalism, printing Priestley and Macintosh, and preaching democracy; in 1792 his group brought out *The Patriot*, a democratic journal voluble about Alfred, the Norman Yoke, Locke, and French Ideas.[25]

All this while, as indeed till the end, Priestley felt the pressure of Lavoisier's rejection of phlogiston, though it took him some time to see how complete the challenge was. In his one surviving letter to Lavoisier he dealt only with objections to his phlogistic theory of respiration. By 1782, however, he realised that the whole theory was being assaulted, and he went on throughout the rest of his life defending it. He clung to the possibility of changing water into air by heating it in contact with calcareous substances, and argued that mixtures of 'inflammable and common airs', repeatedly fired by electric sparks, produced water.[26]

Why did he fail to grasp the significance of Lavoisier's work? From one angle the answer is easy. The phlogiston theory had so long been entwined with his world outlook that he could not detach it and view it in a critical perspective. But certainly the full answer is more complex. He was aware that different sorts of inflammable airs existed.

If you get different acids from the inflammable air made from sulpher and water, that made from marine acid and copper (for I would avoid iron on account of its plumbago and carbon), and that made from charcoal and water: – I say, if those acids are different (suppose, according to my notions, vitriolic, marine, and fixed air), them, will you not be obliged to admit that there is not one inflammable but many inflammables, which opinion you now think as heterodox as the Athanasian system. However, there are wonderful resources in the dispute about phlogiston, by which either party can evade, so that I am less sanguine than you are in hopes of seeing it terminated. [To KEIR probably 1789][27]

He certainly had not lost his experimental skills. Clearly at the back of his mind was a system of thought which felt the phlogiston theory more useful than the *principe oxygine*. Later we shall try to find out what that system was.

The Dissenters were pressing for a repeal of the Corporation and Test Acts that inflicted disabilities on them. In 1788 Priestley printed a strong sermon against the slave trade; in November 1789 he set out the line to be taken by Dissenters in connection with a third application to Parliament and the rights they should claim in the future. In December, meetings were held by Dissenters all over the country. In reply the Church mobilised its forces; Spencer Madan attacked Priestley in particular; on 1 March Members of Parliament were circularised with extracts from his works aimed at showing him as a dangerous firebrand. Fox, who was to propose the motion for the repeal, had to deal with the charges. Price, a supporter of the American revolt and of the revolution beginning in France, preached in November 1789 a sermon *On the Love of Our Country* on the anniversary of the Revolution of 1688–9. Then a powerful lead against the Dissenters was given by Burke, who had been a friend of Priestley. The political prints depicted Lindsey and Priestley in the same pulpit delivering a violent speech or being harried by demons on their way to hell; Sally Priestley made a collection of them. Scurrilous attacks in verse and prose proliferated. In January 1790 three men tried to break into the Priestley house and fired a pistol at a maid. Fox's motion was rejected. Burke published his *Reflections on the Revolution in France, and on the Proceedings in certain Societies in London relative to that Event*. With Priestley in mind he could not resist a chemical metaphor:

The wild *gas*, the fixed air, is plainly broke loose: but we ought to suspend our judgment until the first effervescence is a little subsided, till the liquor is cleared, and until we see something deeper than the agitation of a troubled and frothy surface.

As the French Revolution advanced, the situation grew worse. Priestley was a thorough sympathiser with what was happening in France. When the fleeing King was caught and imprisoned, he remarked to Lindsey, 'Our joy on his capture, cannot be described.' The radicals of Birmingham decided to get together. On 29 June Priestley wrote to London, 'We are forming a Constitutional Society here similar to that in Manchester.' A dinner was to be held on 14 July. Then a few copies of a handbill were found in an inn (under the tables) and in two factories with the statement:

But on the 14th of this month, prove to the political sycophants of the day, that You reverence the Olive Branch; that You *will* sacrifice to public Tranquillity, till the Majority *shall* exclaim, *The peace of Slavery is worse than the War of Freedom*. Of that moment let Tyrants beware.[28]

The origin of the handbill is obscure, but it may have originated from the group in Hackney, the homeground of Price, who were ardent in their support of the French Revolution. In any event it served as excuse for an outbreak of violence, in which Priestley's home was wrecked.

Church-and-King crowds and hired mobs had been appearing from 1790, directed against the Jacobins, especially in provincial towns and urbanised villages. What happened in Birmingham was the manipulation of a traditional mob by the Birmingham Tories; indeed, some of the mob shouted 'No Popery', others were workers who had turned Tory against Jacobin employers. The building-up of emotional bias against 'Traitors', however, went back to the days of the American revolt when the small vanguard group of Dissenters, intellectuals, and radical industrialists were denounced for siding with the enemy. In fact Birmingham, with its host of small workshops, every man 'stinking of train-oil and emery', was the sort of place where one would expect strong artisan Jacobinism; and indeed the 1791 riots did not crush the democratic movement. In November 1792 artisans organised a society with Sheffield help and became quite active.

But Priestley had been effectively exiled. He found time to write *The Duty of Forgiveness of Injuries*, a discourse intended to be delivered soon after the riots in Birmingham (1791), and following his flight he sent a letter:

July 19, 1791

To the Inhabitants of the town of Birmingham.
My Late Townsmen and Neighbours,

You have destroyed the most truly valuable and useful apparatus of philosophical instruments that perhaps any individual, in this or any other country, was ever possessed of, in my use of which I annually spent large sums with no pecuniary view whatever, but only for the advancement of Science, for the benefit of my country and mankind. You have destroyed the Library corresponding to that apparatus, which no money can re-purchase except in the course of time. But what I feel far more, you have destroyed manuscripts which have been the result of the laborious study of many years, and which I shall never be able to recompose; and this has been done to one who never did, or imagined, you any harm.

In this business we are the sheep and you are the wolves. We will preserve our character and hope you will change yours. At all events we return you blessings for curses, and hope that you shall soon return to that industry and those sober manners for which the inhabitants of Birmingham were formerly distinguished.

Yours faithfully J. PRIESTLEY.

He received messages of support from the Dissenters in Great Yarmouth, the French Academy of Sciences (through Condorcet), and the Society of the Friends of the Constitution 'sitting at the Jacobins, Paris', the members of his New Meeting Congregation at Birmingham, the Congregation of the Mill-Hill Chapel at Leeds, the Committee of the Revolution Society in London, the Committee of Dissenters in Yorkshire, the Philosophical Society at Derby, an Assembly of Dissenting Ministers at Exeter, and the Students of New College, Hackney. The Derby Society suggested that he should leave theology for science:

Almost all great minds, in all ages of the world, who have endeavoured to benefit mankind, have been persecuted by them. Galileo, for his philosophical discoveries, was imprisoned by the inquisition; and Socrates found a cup of hemlock his reward for teaching there is one God. Your enemies, unable to conquer your arguments by reason, have had recourse to violence. They have hallooed upon you the dogs of unfeeling ignorance and of frantic fanaticism. They have kindled fires like those of the inquisition, not to illuminate the truth, but, like the dark lanthorn of the assassin, to light the murderer to his prey. Your philosophical friends, therefore, hope that you not again risk your person among a people whose bigotry renders them incapable of instruction. They hope you will leave the unfruitful fields of polemical theology, and cultivate that philosophy of which you may be called the father, and which, by inducing the world to think and reason, will silently marshal mankind against delusion, and, with greater certainty, overturn the empire of superstition[30]

This Address was signed and transmitted by Erasmus Darwin as president of the society. But Priestley could only ignore their appeal. Polemical theology was for him a necessary aspect of the fight for a truly human society and was inseparable from the quest for truth in science. Amusingly, the Address was logically in the key of Hartleian notions about the steady inevitable movement towards perfection; but Priestley was being true to the spirit of those notions in holding that he and all good men must fight for the advance.

He went to Hackney, where William Vaughan provided his family with a refuge. William had been at Warrington, like his brother John, who acted as Priestley's agent after his emigration. The college at Hackney was much to Priestley's heart. The *London Chronicle* of 3 July 1787 had thus announced its foundation:

The Dissenters are establishing an University of their own. A large house and extensive grounds have been purchased at Hackney, for 5,600*l*, to which a wing is to be added, and they have 9000*l*. in anonymous benefactor has just sent them 500*l*., for which their gratitude is expressed in the newspapers. The expense of board, lodging and tuition for each session are 60 guineas to such as are not on the foundation.[31]

From 1791 to 1794 Priestley was in London; but as we should expect his scientific work made no advances. *Experiments on the Generation of Air from Water* (1793) was largely a reprint of earlier papers, and *Heads of Lectures* (1794) tried to set out his general views without fresh experiments. His strength of character, however, was in no way weakened by his difficulties and the cold-shouldering he met from many Fellows of the Royal Society. But he was disheartened enough to decide on emigrating. Also his friends urged him to leave an England where the political situation was worsening in case he should share the fate of other arrested radicals. (T. F. Palmer, a convert of Priestley and Lindsey, with a unitarian congregation at Dundee, was sentenced to seven years' deportation for being associated with a publication that called the war-taxation extravagant and asked for short parliaments and universal suffrage.)

In America he settled at Northumberland, five days' journey up the Susquehanna, where his wife died on 17 September aged 52. By 1797 he had re-established his laboratory, even if inadequately. He now wrote a dozen more theological works (including the four-volume completion of his *General History of the Christian Church*), two pamphlets, one of which dealt with 'the Case of Poor Emigrants', and some 40 papers on experiments – more than twice the number of previous papers, but much poorer in quality. He kept up his wide correspondence and knew of the work of Beddoes, Davy, Volta, Rumford, Cruikshank and others, within a year of publication.

More than ever do I now regret the loss of the *Lunar Society*, where I spent so many happy hours, and for which I found no substitute even in London. Here I am quite isolated and I promise myself, when my house and laboratory shall be erected, to direct as much time to philosophical pursuits as ever I have done. [To WITHERING, October 1795][32]

At Northumberland he felt himself in a provincial town, with Philadelphia as his London. He wanted to play the internationally active part he had played for so many years, but was now definitely out of the advanced scientific world. He tried to re-establish contact, vainly, with a public letter of challenge to the French Chemists in 1796. In March 1795 he had written to Wedgwood, 'I have repeated my experiments on *the generation of air from water* in such a manner as to remove, I think, every objection that can be made to them, and I am pursuing them still further.' He eagerly sought for any weak points (of which there were many) in his opponents' case (*e.g.* its confusion of water with the production of inflammable air), and he seized on Cruickshank's explanation of his own production of inflammable air from ferrosoferric oxide. Cruikshank took the air (correctly) to be an oxide of carbon; and Priestley argued that the experiment destroyed the claims of the new chemists that inflammable air necessarily arose from a decomposition of water. But he over-valued such points and did not realise that the significance of the Lavoisier positions lay, not in any particular explanation of experiments, but in a new conception of what chemistry was.[33]

However, he had also turned to botany – though he wrote in 1795: 'Were I a young man, I should certainly, especially in this new world, apply to Botany and natural history in general; but it is too late in life for me to engage in new pursuits.'[34] He attacked Erasmus Darwin's use of his work on photosynthesis to support a theory of spontaneous generation and produced evidence to show that the 'green matter' of the early observations had not been spontaneously generated.[35] He also made comments on hearing and on dreams. He rejected a professorship of chemistry at the University of Pennsylvania and the presidency of the American Philosophical Society. In his first years of emigration he was not without his political troubles. Pickering, Secretary of State under Adams, wanted to deport him under the Aliens Act, but he won through. In the spring of 1796 he delivered a set of discourses on the Evidences of Christianity in the new church of the Universalists at Philadelphia, before Adams and many other impotant figures. Under Jefferson he could feel quite happy and was consulted by various highly-placed persons including the President. He wrote, 'I now, for the first time in my life (and I shall soon enter my 70th year), find myself in any degree of favour with the government of the country in which I have lived, and I hope I shall die in the same pleasing situation.' Active till the last, he died quietly in 1804.[36]

2 Priestley and Hartley

The work of David Hartley played so important a role in Priestley's thinking that we need to know at least its general lines. Hartley was the son of a clergyman of Armley in Yorkshire. Born in August 1705, he was educated at a private school and in 1720 entered Jesus College, Cambridge, where he became a Fellow. Unable to accept the 39 Articles he abandoned the clerical profession and turned to medicine. After practising at Newark, Bury St. Edmunds, and London, he spent his last years at Bath. He published many medical papers especially on the stone, the disease of which he himself died in August 1757.[1] His *Observations on Man,* the result of sixteen years' careful work, was published in 1749. His son wrote in 1801:

He did not expect that it would meet with any general or immediate reception in the philosophical world, or even that it would be much read or understood; neither did it happened otherwise than as he had expected. But at the same time he did ascertain an expectation that, at some distant period, it would become the adopted system of future philosophers. That period now seems to be approaching.[2]

Hartley had studied optics, statics and the like under Hales, Smith (then master of Trinity College, Cambridge), and other members of the Royal Society; in his medical work he keenly observed people; and he spent much spare time in studying history – he was a friend of Nairne, historian of ancient Rome. From Newton, whom he deeply admired, he drew his theory of vibrations. One of his interests was the reformation of the language, and he welcomed proposals for universal and philosophical languages and dictionaries. While he admired the verse of Pope and Young, he hated poems on love and beauty. The first sketch of his *Observations* was made in Latin.

His great contribution was the theory of the Association of Ideas. Locke and Hume had used a similar theory, but in a less precise way. Where Hume saw only customary connections at work, Hartley saw a mechanism explaining all mental and emotional processes. He felt that he was applying to the inner world the same sort of laws as Newton had applied to the outer, and that he was carrying out the work which Newton had desiderated in his *Principia* when he said that he wished it were possible to:

derive the rest of the phenomena of Nature by the same kind of reasoning from mechanical principles, for I am induced by many reasons to suspect that they may all depend upon certain forces by which the particles of bodies, by some cause hitherto unknown, are either mutually attracted towards one another, and cohere in regular figures, or are repelled and recede from one another.[3]

Hartley hoped to find an inner law of cohesion corresponding to the outer law of gravitational attraction and as amenable to mechanical description. In the eighteenth century any demonstration of regularity in phenomena was seized on by religious apologists, whether orthodox Christian or Deist, as proof of a contriving deity. Newton was seen as the great bulwark against atheisim; and Hartley, in seeking a mechanist theory of the moral world, could feel himself a champion of religion.

By the mechanism of human actions, I mean that each action results from the previous circumstances of body and mind, in the same manner and with the same certainty, as other effects of from their mechanical causes.[4]

And he thought that by establishing the existence of such a mechanism he reconciled 'the prescience of God with the free will of man'. The thinker from whom he drew his association-thesis was not so much Locke as the Rev. John Gay, who set out his ideas in a dissertation printed by Law on his translation of King's *Essay on the Origin of Evil*, 1732. Gay saw the aim of all our actions as 'private Happiness', but the means that we used was Association. Through it we arrived at Resting Places or acquired principles. Thus, he linked the idea of pleasure with certain objects and

B

the association remained when its cause was 'quite forgot'.[5] And so on with money, knowledge, fame. A moral sense and public affections were gained through observation or imitation of others.

Hartley rejected the position of Hutcheson that our moral sense is instinctive, or the position of the mathematical Platonists, Clarke and Cudworth, that it is founded in the eternal relation of things. In the first part of his *Observations* he sketched out a materialist system to explain the mechanism of sensation. He drew on Hobbes to connect the mechanism with the white medullary substance of the brain, in which the minute particles receive and reproduce vibrations from sensible objects.[6] Here he was also influenced by Newton. The responses in the brain he named Vibratiuncles or Miniatures; and ideas he saw as born out of associated sensations and growing complex by accretion. However, he shrank from endowing matter with thought as Hobbes and even Locke did; so he suggested a sort of parallelism between brain and mind.[7] Descartes indeed had pronounced animals nothing but machines, though he did little to construct a mechanist system of physiology: that was initiated in the eighteenth century by A. van Haller, while Julien de la Mettrie wrote, anonymously, a book with the title *Man a Machine*. Hartley as a physician may have been influenced by such trends, but the physiological side of his theory was the least important.[8]

Since, he believed, people were moulded by circumstances and not made up from the start in some fixed way by inherited or god-implanted characteristics, they could be directed by a change of circumstances along better lines, and ultimately perfected. That is, have their egoistic and anti-social qualities eliminated. He reversed the traditional Christian position of a decline from Edenic days, which could be checked only by a total submission of the will to Christ, and held that 'Association has a tendency to rescue the state of those who have eaten the Tree of Knowledge of Good and Evil, back to a paradisical one'.[9] Since we are all essentially similar and equally exposed to the steady action of the whole of things, we tend to find our 'particular differences' smoothed away. 'If one be happy, all must.' This general happiness was the natural goal of a providentially designed world in which the association principle worked for the good of all. 'Our Passions and Affections can be no more than Aggregates of simple ideas united by Association,' and out of such aggregations came the moral sense, which was not inborn.

Sensation, then, was the basis. From it we moved upwards by associating pleasure with ever wider, loftier, worthier objects till we reached God, the totality. (There was no place for Christ in such a system, unless he was viewed as the teacher of a constantly socialising principle, which, however acted by its own nature and did not need such a teacher in order to come into existence or to continue.) But what had gone wrong that the principle did not work harmoniously in all persons and at all phases of history? What cankers arose to arrest pleasure at unworthy or evil objects? This point was not squarely faced; but Hartley did deal with the problem of undoing and changing a bad knot of associations. The way was to reach back to the point of arrest break the perverted connection and start afresh on the upward trend.

The Affections and Passions should be analysed into their simple compounding Parts, by reversing the Steps of the Associations which concur to form them. For thus we learn how to cherish and improve good ones, check and root out such as are mischievous and immoral, and how to suit our Manner of Life, in some tolerable Measure, to our intellectual and religious Wants.[10]

These aspects of Hartley's thoughts had a fundamental and lasting effect on Wordsworth with his creed of a return to Nature as a cure for the evils inflicted by a corrupt society. The sufferer was to be 'remanded' to Nature to 'go back as far as occasion will permit to Nature and to solitude' and 'measure back the tracks of life he has trod'. (Wordsworth, however, still relied on a 'wise passiveness'; the same doctrine of return to the point of arrest or cankering appears in Freudian theory and method, but in a more complex, dramatising, and dynamic way.)[11]

Hartley in fact tended to impose a rigid moral attitude rather than any creed of tranquil returns to nature in meditative communion. To gain 'the Maximum of the sensible Pleasures, even those of Taste', we must not abandon ourselves to them, but must 'restrain them, and make them subject to Benevolence, Piety, and the Moral Sense'.[12] Any failure to do so is to obstruct Providence, which has worked out the upward-moving system as the moral mechanism for civilising men.

After Sensation comes Imagination, then the pleasures and pains of Ambition (Hume's Social Reactions). Virtue is born from the desire for praise and approval. Pleasing Consciousness and Self-approbation 'rise up in the mind of the person who thinks himself possessed of virtuous qualities, exclusively of any direct explicit consideration of advantage likely to accrue to himself'.[13] Self-interest in its gross form becomes refined and then takes on a rational aspect, which merges with the 'abstract Desire for Happiness'. Sympathy, Compassion, Mercy, and Sociability are early generated by Association; the selfish element is slowly eliminated and we are led on to Theopathy or the Love of God. Finally comes the highest stage, the Moral Sense. Incidentally Hartley stressed the association of impressions (made by written words or uttered sounds on the sense of sight or hearing) with the corresponding ideas, and tried to develop a theory of language and of writing. The rigid moral attitudes came out in a wholesale condemnation of the Polite Arts except when 'consecrated to religious purposes'. He says, 'It is evident that most kinds of music, painting, and poetry have close connexions with vice, particularly with the vices of intemperance and lewdness,' the aristocratic vices. Also, 'The arts are apt to excite vanity, self-conceit, and mutual flatteries, in their votaries.' Not that the sciences are much better, since 'nothing can exceed the vain-glory, self-conceit, arrogance, emulation, and envy, that are found in the eminent professors of the sciences, mathematics, philosophy, and even divinity itself'.[14]

The contemplation of Nature, however, is different. But it is characteristic that we do not find a moral or aesthetic attitude here dominant. Nature is admirable because it is equated with Mechanism. The ideas of uniformity and variety in combination, called up by natural scenes, produce pleasure because of their intimate connection with the idea of Adaptability to Ends, which is aroused by similar properties in mechanical works and contrivances.[15]

As usual in such systems there is an unstated assumption of varying levels in the action of the principle. From the higher levels we can change the circumstances in the lower ones and thus mould the circumstances that mould us. The upward trend is thereby assured. Priestley, in taking over the system, took over the assumptions. The contradiction lay in the belief that the action of the mechanism, left to itself, would automatically turn sensation into a moral sense and achieve a universal humanity on the highest rational level, and in the moral insistence that every effort must be made to drop the lower pleasures and that men must struggle consciously to put themselves in accord with the mechanism.[16] Hartley had no notion of the number of pitfalls in such a statement as the following: Rational Assent to any Proposition 'is a readiness to affirm it to be true, proceeding from a close association of the ideas suggested by the proposition, with the idea, or internal feeling, belonging to the word Truth; or of the terms of the proposition with the word Truth'. Hume would have enjoyed tearing such a thesis to pieces. The apparently objective action of the mechanism proves to have a sheer solipsism at its core, a purely subjective criterion of truth. Amusingly, the one point at which Hartley altogether drops his optimistic belief in the providential working of the system is when he looks out at the education methods of his world. They 'threaten ruin and dissolution to the present states of Christendom'.[17] Priestley took over from Hartley his scheme of Association as the principle of inner movement and development; and he too felt that the scheme ensured a blithe forward progress. In 1782 he cried:

The morning is upon us, and we cannot doubt that the light will increase, and extend itself more and more unto the perfect day. Happy are those who contribute to diffuse the pure light of this everlasting gospel.[18]

The notion of the Second Coming and the Millenary Rule of the Saints is secularised into that of human perfectibility brought about by the providential workings of the Association Principle. The Everlasting Gospel here has its close links with that of Blake, though in Blake the understanding of revolutionary process has become incomparably more complex. Priestley's optimism is, however, in its turn much more complex than that of Hartley; for he links it directly and closely with contemporary struggles in the political, social, and cultural fields, and does not give a merely general application. Thus, in 1790, stimulated by the French Revolution, in *The proper Objects of Education in the present State of the World*, he made a bold statement of his hopes, which stirred the official world into thoughts of prosecution:

While so favourable a wind is abroad, let every young mind expand itself, catch the rising gale, and partake of the glorious enthusiasm; the great objects of which are the flourishing state of science, arts, manufactures and commerce, the extinction of wars, with all the calamities incident to mankind from them, the abolishing of all useless distinctions, which were the offspring of a barbarous age (producing an absurd haughtiness in some, and a base servility in others), and a general release from all such taxes, and burdens of every kind, as the public good does not require. In short, to make government as beneficial, and as little expensive and burdensome, as possible.[19]

We may note the anticlimax as the buoyant fervour of the opening drops down to the hope of tax-reduction. In this sort of thing Priestley was typical of the radicals of his day, who on the one hand expressed an anarchist utopian goal in which the State was reduced to something like impotence, with a completely free blossoming of all human potentialities; and on the other hand reduced their programme to a liberal *laisser-faire* programme of triumphantly expanding capitalism. The same mixture of ideas and impulses can be found, from a different angle, in Paine.

Again, though Priestley showed little signs of appreciating art or poetry,

he lacked the bleak puritanism of Hartley. In early years he wrote verses.
He composed *To Mr. Annet on his new Short Hand*; and his *Memoirs* say
that Mrs. Barbauld was inspired by his example. Indeed, it was perhaps
the pressure of his many other interests that kept him away from poetry;
for when he had enforced leisure during his journey to America he did
much reading of verse. He wrote to Lindsey from New York
(6 June 1794):

The confinement in the ship would not have been disagreeable if I could
have *written* with convenience, but I could do little more than read. I read
the whole of the Greek Testament, and the Hebrew Bible as far as the
first Book of Samuel; and, I think, with more satisfaction than ever. I
also read through Hartley's second volume, and, for amusement, I had
several books of voyages, and Ovid's Metamorphoses, which I read through
I always admired his Latin versification. If I had a Virgil, I should have
read him through, too. I read a great deal of Buchanan's [Latin] poems,
and some of Petrarch *de remediis,* and Erasmus's Dialogues; also Peter
Pindar's poems, which Mr. Lyon had with him, and which pleased me
much more than I expected. He is Paine in verse. Though it was particularly inconvenient to write long hand, I composed about as much as
will make two sermons on the cause of infidelity, which will make a proper
addition to the volume of my discourses. If I do not print them here, I will
send you a copy. Now that I have access to the first volume of Hartley, in
the fine edition Mrs. Lindsey gave me, I think I can improve what I wrote.
The second volume I had in the ship, was an odd volume of the set that
was destroyed in the riot.[20]

We see how incessantly active he had to be. Despite all his reading and
writing on shipboard, he had time to observe nature in an unfamiliar
setting:

We had many things to amuse us in the passage; as the sight of some fine
mountains of ice; water-spouts, which are very uncommon in these seas;
flying fishes, porpoises, whales, and sharks, of which we caught one;
luminous sea-water, &c. I also amused myself with trying the heat of the
water at different depths, and made other observations, which suggest
various experiments, which I shall prosecute whenever I get my apparatus
at liberty. We had some very stormy weather, and one gust of wind as
sudden and violent as, perhaps, was ever known. If it had not been for the
passengers, many of the sails had been lost.

The remarks on his reading and writing during the voyage show how, even
at this late stage, he was still deeply attached to Hartley. His own enthusiasm for science was boundless. He felt sure that it would end all
corruptions in religion and political life, and that 'in this enlightened age',
the attempts to hold up its advance would only make 'the final ruin' of the
establishment more 'complete and glorious'.

It was ill policy in Leo the X to patronize polite literature. He was cherishing
an enemy in disguise. And the English hierarchy (if there is anything un-
sound in its constitution) has equal reason to tremble even at an air pump,
or an electrical machine.[21]

He thus developed on Hartley's positions in two ways. He used them to
set out a thorough-going materialism and to reject everything in
Christianity that did not have a direct socialising tendency. In 1775 he
reprinted Hartley's work, leaving out most of the anatomical and theological
matcrial, and adding three dissertations. Then he published his own
extensions of Hartley's theory, *Disquisitions Relating to Matter and Spirit*
and *The Doctrine of Philosophical Necessity Illustrated* (1777). He accepted
the total materiality of man, but did not oppose his materialism to religion;
rather he identified it with 'the system of *pure Revelation*' and opposed
it to that of 'a vain and absurd philosophy'. So he set out to prove that
matter did not deserve the low rating it had got in almost all philosophies.
So far from being dull, inert, impenetrable, as opposed to thought, it
owned inherent powers of attraction and repulsion, and from these came
its so-called solidity and resistance. Thus the 'reproach of matter is wiped
off'. Thought and sensation were to be found only in connection with an
organised system of matter; the brain was the seat of thought, but the
brain's vibrations were not themselves the perceptions; rather the brain,
'besides its vibrating power, has super-added to it a percipient or sentient
power, likewise'. He reproved Locke for clinging to an immaterial soul.
The idea of immortality had been imported into Christianity 'from the
Oriental and Greek philosophy, which in many respects altered and
debased the true Christian system'. The idea of the soul as a substance
distinct from the body was pure heathenism.[22]

    In these arguments his method was historical. He pointed out that the
idea of pure immateriality was a modern concoction – 'really an upstart
thing, and a nonentity'. The ancients thought of the immaterial as 'only
a *finer kind* of what we should now call matter'. The Scriptures knew
nothing of a separable soul.[23] He thus used Hartleyism for an uncom-
promising rejection of everything not simply social and materialist in
Christianity as a mere 'idolatry': the incarnation, the atonement, the
trinity, the divinity of Jesus, and so on, were all damnable corruptions.
As the mechanism of Association grew more perfect, all such nonsense
and distortion would be ended, and Christianity would regain 'its primitive
glory and beauty'. (Hartley had suggested that the moral sense could and
should operate 'without any express Recollection of the Hopes and Fears

of another World', but he would have blenched at Priestley's ruthless cleansing of the Temple.)[24] The only apparently irrational element which Priestley, like Milton and Hobbes, accepted, was the idea of a Resurrection at the Last Day. But he held that the revived persons had been well and truly dead in all respects; and the recomposition of the decomposed by the Being who first effected the composition was done, not by any miracle, but by some natural (chemical) law unknown to us.

In his doctrine of Philosophical Necessity he meant to deny the possibility of arbitrary caprice or of chance decisions: we act always by motive. This viewpoint, required by his general philosophical position, had for him the added value in that he saw it as the opposite of Calvinism with its Predestination. Calvinism, attributing everything to God's Will, made human efforts to change things impious or futile; Philosophical Necessity urged men to change circumstances so that they themselves might be formed in more perfect ways. That was how he saw it all; but in fact one aspect of his position laid as little stress on effort as did Calvinism, and encouraged submission to the motions of a universe in 'all things, even to their minutest circumstances' . . . 'always for the best of purposes'. But as with Hartley, though even more strongly, the essential direction of his thought was towards arousing men to take control of circumstance and perfect themselves with all possible speed. Man, he declared, now knows that 'it depends entirely upon himself whether' the temper and disposition of his mind 'be improved or not'. And so he considered his creed of Necessity to provide a cheerful and stimulating view as opposed to the gloomy one of Calvinism. He did not shrink from calling himself a materialist. Thus in April 1778 he wrote to the Rev. C. Rotherham:

I was an Arian till I went to Leeds, and my Materialism is but of late standing, though you see that I now consider the doctrine of the *soul* to have been imported into Christianity, and to be the foundation of the capital corruptions of our religion.[25]

His positions in history and politics followed from his creed of Necessity, and in many ways reposed on Locke, Russell and Sidney;[26] society and its system of government were instruments of providence. The economic basis of progress lay in the continual division of labour, which he saw as an endless subdivision and extension of knowledge and human powers. As he set out these ideas in his *Essay on the First Principles of Government, and on the Nature of Political, Civil and Religious Liberty*, 1768, he was anticipating some of Adam Smith's arguments published in 1776. He distinguished political and civil liberty: the first gave one a voice in government or a vote; the second was 'the power over their own actions which the members of the state reserve to themselves, and which their own officers must not infringe'. He expanded Locke's thesis on the right to revolution. If a government failed to promote the general utility, the people must resume their natural liberties and punish or remove their servants. The utilitarian principle was 'the good and happiness of the members, that is the majority of the members of any state'. But 'persons of considerable fortune' or those best educated were those naturally eligible for highest offices; 'dependants' should have no vote in the election of chief magistrates. There is thus an odd discrepancy between the enthusiastic insistence on the right and the need for revolutionary resistances, and the conventional ideas as to what constituted a reasonable social system; between the dream of equal perfectibility and the acceptance of inequalities.

Civil liberty, Priestley said, gave a man a 'constant feeling of his own power and importance; and is the foundation of his indulging in a free, bold, and manly turn of thinking, unrestrained by the most distant idea of control'. He pushed his libertarian views to the extent of objecting to public education, which could be used to create uniform and stereotyped attitudes and reactions. 'One method of education would produce only one kind of men; but the greatest excellence of human nature consists in the variety of which it is capable'[27] – a point of view that was scarcely in accord with the Hartleian concept of the association principle as working to smoothe away all 'particular differences'. Priestley, for all his strong social feelings, had the weakness of bourgeois atomic individualism. 'It is an universal maxim, that the more liberty is given to everything which is in a state of growth, the more perfect it will become.' Liberty is there conceived in a vacuum, and the dialectics of real growth ignored. This side of Priestley led on to Bentham and Mill.[28] He had rejected the Scottish thinkers, Reid, Beattie, Oswald; but there was much he could have learned from Scottish thought on the deep contradictions of the bourgeois industrialising trends that he saw as wholly rational and good. For instance, he might well have pondered what Adam Ferguson said of industrialism and the division of labour: 'We make a nation of Helots, and have no free citizens.' Even Adam Smith had seen that factory work stunted the worker: it 'corrupts the courage of the mind. . . . It corrupts even the activity of his body.' But Priestley, like Paine, was too deeply rooted in the world of the small producer, the craftsman in the first tentative stages of industrial organisation, to grasp what was really happening; he was thus able to cling to his libertarian dogmas.

There is indeed at times something ludicrous when he descends from general ideas to their application. After arguing well that countries with religious toleration are the happiest and most prosperous, he decides that there is little to fear 'in this enlightened age' from the extravagances of zeal or popery; and so he suggests as an immediate step the reduction of the 39 Articles of the Established Church to 38. His all-too-simple optimism defeats his genuine quest for historical sources and patterns.

Lectures on History and General Policy was written for use at Warrington, but published in enlarged form, after he had read Gibbon and Adam Smith, in 1788. He saw history as 'a progress towards a state of greater perfection'. It supplied the data for political science. The great period was that of the Revival of Learning (the Renascence) when the power of the Papacy was broken, manufactures rose, and there was an increase in politeness and humanity. Again, 1688 gave a great stimulus to 'science, commerce, riches, power, and, I may add, happiness'. The reading of Smith increased his aversion to any form of governmental interference. Education and enlightenment would teach the rich how to use their wealth for 'the good of the whole'. Just give free scope to those forces. War? He hoped that societies would learn by experience to avoid 'the ruinous expences and devastation of *war*'. Expenses, we note, came first; war was an abomination by giving pretexts for taxes. Anyway, 'as the world advances in civilisation, and national animosity abates, war becomes less distressing to peaceable individuals who do not bear arms'.[29]

His social and political views were thus typical of those of the other radicals of the day, even of Paine. We find rather trivial applications of a petty-bourgeois or small-producer idea of what best provides elbow-room and a basis for comfortable profit without interference from the state (which is seen essentially as an outmoded feudal survival) – and at the same time a great sweep of large-scale ideas, urged with revolutionary fervour, that imply a regenerated earth of peace and brotherhood.

We might say that he needed his Christian creed, purged of all he considered irrational, because of its promise of the redemption (that is, perfectibility) of the human race. That promise helped him to disregard the unresolved conflicts in his Hartleian positions and to concentrate the revolutionary fervour. Especially, his study of Biblical Prophecies enabled him to preserve intact his sense of impending convulsions and vast social changes. In the letter of August 1771 to Lindsey about photosynthesis, which was cited above, immediately before the scientific report of the way in which vegetation changes deadly airs to life-giving ones, he breaks into a prophecy of imminent dooms:

. . . I hope I have not been rightly informed when I was told that, in consequence of some steps taken by the Bishop (I think) of Lincoln your intended application to Parliament [against the Liturgy and the Thirty-nine Articles] is dropped, and that nothing more will be done in the business. If this is true, in how striking a light doth it shew the danger of such comp-licated establishments! Nothing, however, can deprive you of the honour of having endeavoured to bring about a reformation, and by posterity you will be remembered with gratitude and respect.
To me everything looks like the approach of that dismal catastrophe described, I may say predicted, by Dr. Hartley, in the conclusion of his Essay, and I shall be looking for the downfall of Church and State together. I am really expecting some very calamitous, but finally glorious, events. Happy they who will be found watching in the way of their duty![30]

He continued to interpret the social upheavals of his time in terms of world-end and regeneration. On 12 August 1795 he wrote to Lindsey from America about hopes of peace:

This would be a most desirable event, indeed, but I fear a greater blessing than the state of the world will autorize us to expect. I cannot help being sensibly impressed with the language of prophecy, though happily we cannot tell how long the evil day may be delayed or (for the elects' sake) shortened.[37]

Again on 1 November 1798:

Though we are always apt to magnify present appearances, I have little doubt but that the great prophecies relating to the permanent and happy state of the world, are in the way of fulfilment; but the preceding period of calamity may be of long continuance. The termination of the temporal power of the Pope [by the people's proclamation of the Roman Republic on 15 February 1798], and the destruction of the monarchy that made him a temporal power, shew us pretty clearly *where we are,* and what we have next to look for. I rejoice to hear of something respecting the Jews. Whatever it be, it must prepare the way for their restoration. The French, it is said, have it in view, in consequence of some proposals they have made to them; and that they have no view to the fulfilment of prophecy, is a favourable circumstance. We have just heard of Buonaparte's safe arrival at Alexandria [taken by assault, 5 July 1798], and part of his force at Scande-roon. Whatever be the object of that expedition, it seems to be hazardous. However, great things may come of it, and those not intended by the French.[32]

Because of his dependence on revolutionary change as a necessary event to usher in the millenium, he remained friendly throughout to the French Revolution. There was no question of high hopes followed by disillusion-ment. Though a man of peace and non-interference, he felt no repugnance to the terror or the wars in defence of the French Republic. He would certainly have preferred things to have developed without violence; but the advent of violence did not affect what he felt to be the essential significance of the events. When Condorcet sent him in 1791 the sympathy of the French Academy of Science for his sufferings in the Birmingham riots, he replied warmly:

> I am more than consoled for my losses in finding that the members of the Academy of Sciences have done me the honour to interest themselves in my affairs, and especially in observing that the friends of philosophy are, what they ever ought to be, the friends of general liberty. . . .
> I shall not fail, while my life and my faculties are continued to me, to resume my philosophical pursuits, and endeavour to shew our common enemies that a genuine love of science, and of liberty, is inextinguishable, except with life, and that unreasonable and wicked opposition tends to animate, rather than depress, the mind that is penetrated with it.[33]

On 21 September 1792 (which he himself described as the '4th year of Liberty') he replied to M. Rabaud on the invitation to sit in the National Convention for the Department of L'Orme:

> Such an office is certainly at this time of the utmost importance on the theatre of the world, as the peace and happiness, not only of your country, but of all Europe, and perhaps of the whole human race, are very particularly interested in everything which may be decided in that Assembly; but my imperfect knowledge of your language, local circumstances, and the important duties of my present situation, prevent me from accepting your invitation. . . .
> As a minister of religion, the object of my most ardent desires is your happiness. I sincerely pray that the Supreme Being, the Father and Friend of mankind, whose providence directs all events, may destroy the machinations of your enemies, and put an end to the troubles with which you are now agitated, and may He give a speedy and happy establishment to your affairs.[34]

He seems to have made no reference to Lavoisier's fate. However, in his Open Letter to the French Chemists of 15 June 1796, on the theme of Phlogiston, he shows a dislike of the use of force in repressive powers; but he makes his allusion obliquely and ends with his full support, as if to imply that any criticisms were peripheral matters in comparison with his whole-hearted defence of the Revolution:

> As you would not, I am persuaded, have your reign to resemble that of *Robespierre*, few as we are who remain disaffected, we hope you had rather gain us [to Lavoisier's thesis] by persuasion, than silence us by power. . . .
> If you gain as much by your answer to me, as you did by that to Mr. Kirwan [a phlogistinist, who was won over by the French in 1791], your power will be universally established, and there will be no *Vendée* in your dominion.

Differing as we do in this respect, we all agree in our wishes, for the prevalence of *truth*, and also, of peace, is wanted as much for the interests
of philosophy as for those of humanity.[35]

Before we pass on, we may note the multiple interactions of science, art,
and poetry in the eighteenth century. The Hartley–Priestley doctrine much
affected Coleridge and Wordsworth; and experiments with light had strong
effects on poetic imagery as well as on art, most directly on Joseph Wright
of Derby in the field of painting, but in a wide and complex way on the
poets. Turner, who strongly held to the associationist school of philosophy,
seems to have derived many of the ideas and images of *Ulysses Deriding
Polyphemus*, for instance, from Priestley. The shining sea-creatures with
stars on their brows can be traced directly to the *History and Present State
of Discoveries Relating to Vision, Light and Colour* (as John Gage has shown).
The title of this book would have drawn Turner's attention, for he was
well read in works on perspective and light. Priestley writes:

That the *sea* is sometimes luminous, especially when it is put in motion,
by the dashing of oars, or the beating of it against a ship, has been observed
with admiration by a great number of persons. . . . Father Bourzes, in his
voyage to the Indies, in 1704, took particular notice of the luminous appearance of the sea; but though many of the circumstances which he mentions
seemed to point to the true cause of it, viz. the putrescent matter in the
sea, he does not seem to have been aware of it. The light was sometimes so
great, that he could easily distinguish, in the wake of the ship, the particles
that were luminous from those that were not; and they appeared to be
not at all of the same figure. Some of them were like points of light, and
others such as stars appear to the naked eye. Some of them were like globes,
of a line or two in diameter, and others as big as one's hand. . . . Nor only
did the wake of the ship produce this light, but fishes also swimming,
left so luminous a track behind them, that both their size and species might
be distinguished by it. . . . M. le Roi, making a voyage on the Mediterranean,
took notice that, in the day time, the prow of the ship in motion threw up
many small particles, which, falling upon the water, rolled upon the surface
of the sea, for a few seconds, before they mixed with it; and in the night,
the same particles, as he concluded, had the appearance of fire.

Turner's combination of stars, fish, oars and prow makes certain that he
was recalling Priestley; and later in some note on Goethe's *Theory of
Colours*, against two passage on irridescence and incipient putrescence of
fish, he noted 'Ceylon (?) fish' and 'macker(e)l': which seems a reminiscence
of the experiment with boiled mackerel, for the production of luminous
water, which Priestley discusses in the chapter from which the above-cited
passage is taken.[36]

3 *Boscovich and Priestley*

Roger Joseph Boscovich (1711–87) was educated in the Jesuit College in Ragusa (now Dubrovnik), and later at the Collegium in Rome. Passing his doctorate, he entered the Jesuit priesthood in 1744 and began his career as teacher, poet, diplomat, astronomer and scientist. Priestley seems to have come on his work through John Michell, while he was at work on the *History of Optics* in 1772. After that, Boscovich's *Naturalis Philosophiae Theoria* (1758, editions also in 1759 and 1764) was never far from his mind; it fused with the work of Newton and Hartley to produce his mature positions.

Boscovich's basic law was that all phenomena arise from special arrangements and relative displacements of identical point-particles interacting by pairs under an oscillatory law determining their relative accelerations.[1] This law sought to combine as effectively as possible the notions of both the atom and of quantity. The seventeenth century had come to realise the importance of measured quantities; Huygens, Newton, and D. Bernouilli wanted to apply measurement to atoms – but Boscovich was the first after Newton to see how fertile the fusion of the two notions could be.

I have come, in fact, to a unique law of forces that depends on the distances. They are repulsive and increase without limit when distances diminish endlessly, they increase with increasing distances, then vanish and change into attractive forces which increase, and then again diminish, vanish and change again into negative forces; this process is repeated alternately and many times, until, finally, at larger distances – within reach of our senses – there exists the attraction which at the beginning increases strongly, and then diminished inversely to the square of the distance.[2]

Thus he felt that he had reached a degree of simplicity and uniformity in nature far beyond anything discovered by Newton. However, the conclusions thus reached were indeed opposite to Newton's. Newton had assumed that the greatest attractive force appears in the contact of particles, and that primary particles were perfectly rigid and hard. Also he did not try to find any reason for it, or interconnection between solidity, impenetrability, extension of bodies, and other properties that he took to be the primary properties of matter; gravitation, fermentation, and cohesion of parts were accepted as general causes of change without further investigation. Boscovich showed that the three Newtonian principles, and also the impenetrability and inextension of elements, 'follow from a unique law of forces represented by a curve "simple in itself" as well as "other general properties of bodies and many special ones" ' (Markovic).[3]

As the founder of atomic physics, he introduced a clear concept of structure into physics and chemistry. Applying the principle of continuity to atomic collisions, he arrived at the notion of atoms, then of point-centres; he thus made point-particles the minimal assumption or model for the mathematics of atomism. The impact of hard surfaces involved a difficult discontinuity; but he sought to overcome this problem by bringing in repulsive forces. He got rid of the intractible and unnecessarily hard nucleus by substituting for it a point-centre of action. His *puncta* or *prima elementa* are not atoms; rather they correspond to the nucleons of modern physics.[4] But they were seen as permanent. The universe consists of *puncta*, with Space as the frame of their spatial relations, Time the succession of their changing spatial patterns. Such a universe had no place for the Newtonian scheme of two kinds of space (one empty, one matter-occupied). The Boscovichian single Space was made up of the spatial relations of the discrete *puncta*; even inertia was made relational and motion was determined in the last resort in relation to the frame of the fixed stars. The system of the *puncta* revealed a universe of four basic situations, which were characterised by attractive or repulsive action, by stable or unstable equilibrium.[5]

The *Theoria* thus provided the first general mathematical theory of atomism; Huygens' ideas had a much more limited range. Also it was the first theory for which it can be claimed that it sought:

1. To treat all the ultimate constituents of matter as *identical*. 2. To employ finite numbers of *point* particles. 3. To eliminate Newtonian mass as a primary quantity, substituting a *kinematic* basis. 4. To postulate a *relational* basis for the mathematical treatment of inertia and of all space and time observations. 5. To propose to derive all physical effects from a *single law*. 6. To eliminate the scale-free similarity property of the Newtonian law, introducing *natural lengths* into continuous laws so as to determine unique equilibrium positions and other scale-fixed properties. 7. To employ a *power series* to represent an observable. [L. L. WHYTE][6]

Boscovich in fact qualitatively predicted phenomena that have been since observed, such as the penetrability of matter by high-speed particles.

We can see then why he so strongly attracted Priestley and stimulated in him the desire to derive all physical and spiritual effects from a single law: giving a much greater precision to the hopes that had been aroused by Newton and Hartley. Here was the Matter he wanted, with a kinematic basis, which he could use to establish a unitary life-process and to attack all dualisms of mind and body. He was attracted by the Boscovician conviction of simplicity and analogy in nature, the presentation of continuity, which seemed to justify the arguments of Leibniz' followers that nothing in nature occurs by jumps.

Newton, drawing on Boyle, had tried to explain chemical facts on the basis of corpuscles or atoms, with different or similar geometrical shapes, subject to universal gravitation. But this thesis fell down when specific reactions were considered. Why should gravitational force, which normally brought about shapeless lumps of matter, at the atomic level beget molecular form constant, regular, and reproducible? But Boscovich could explain elective affinity and constant chemical composition at the molecular level.[7] Most scientists, however, in eighteenth-century England had no interest in fundamental structure; their attention was given to practical experiment. So Boscovich was more or less ignored – though John Michell (1724–93) astronomer and geologist, did comment to Priestley, perhaps soon after 1760 (the year in which he met Boscovich in Cambridge), on the advantages of physical point-centres over hard finite atoms.[8] Certainly Boscovich's ideas sank deep into Priestley's mind and determined many of his approaches to phenomena, though he shrank from saying so with full explicitness. In his century scientists were liable to give us few glimpses into the theoretical background of their experiments and researches; they felt that the correct thing to do was to put down a set of facts and the deductions drawn from them. Their notion of Nature lay behind this procedure; for they felt that nature was rational and that natural processes, rationally approached, should yield up their secrets without theoretical fuss and bother. In fact they were all the while using a complex series of assumptions, questions, expectations, which were born partly from conscious or unconscious theoretical views and partly from the pressures of contemporary culture (including technology). Priestley was no exception, despite his desire to find a single law governing all processes.

It was probably Boscovich rather than Newton that he had in mind when he made the first mathematical formulation about electricity in an experiment that could be repeated and verified: that 'the attraction of electricity is subject to the same laws with that of gravitation' = i.e. it varied proportionately to the inverse square of the distance. But though he was glad to invoke the great name of Newton and suggest that he had found a law of electrical attraction which might prove as fruitful as that of gravitation, he may well have had in mind, in making the discovery, the

Boscovichian application of the same formula to attractive and repulsive forces at the atomic level. The latter use, however, lacked the acceptance of the Newtonian, and he may have considered it premature to attempt a synthesis of gravitational, electrical, and atomic forces – as indeed it was! In any event that sort of unification was what Priestley was looking for and hoping to bring out.[9]

Just when Priestley first read Boscovich cannot be proved. He certainly knew his work well before 1772 when he gave up several pages of *The History of Optics* to his doctrine, and ended with the hope that 'I shall be excused for dwelling so long on this hypothesis on account both of the *novelty* and the *importance* of it. . . .'[10] But that does not necessarily imply that he had only just read the *Theoria*; in 1772 Boscovich's work was still almost unknown in England. The Abbé had visited London in 1760 and been elected into the Royal Society; Boswell mentions that after meeting Samuel Johnson at Reynold's house he expressed astonishment at the Doctor's Latin conversation. He met many persons, including Dolland and Short, the best opticians of the day; Burke and the dramatist Murphy; Reynolds, Richard Wilson, and R. E. Pine (who painted his portrait); and many other fashionable people from Lord Dashwood to Lady Pembroke. Among his sponsors to the Royal Society were the Astronomer Royal, the Keeper of MSS in the British Museum, a Fellow of Trinity, Cambridge, the Secretary of the Royal Society (who had edited Cudworth's *Intellectual System*).[11] He attended several of the Society's meetings and reported on Delisle's statement about the forthcoming Transit of Venus, his paper being printed in the *Transactions* of 1760. Further he met Franklin at Wilson's house. We may be sure that so curious a collector of scientific information as Priestley knew of the visit and the comments it provoked. Michell, we noted, met Boscovich at Cambridge and spoke to Priestley, perhaps not so long after, on the advantages of *puncta* over hard finite atoms. It is extremely likely then that Priestley got hold of the *Theoria* shortly after the visit of Boscovich and avidly devoured it. It certainly played a key part in his development of the notion of matter as active principle, as opposed to prevailing ideas of its inertia and 'deadness'.

Still, his discovery of Michell's ideas does seem to have strengthened his adherence to Boscovichian views and helped him to mature his ideas on the nature of matter. Possibly he needed to brood over the *Theoria* some time before he could see fully how to incorporate its positions in his own world outlook; and Michell may have clarified his mind. He wrote, on 7 March 1773, to the Rev. J. Bretland:

The objections you make to the hypothesis of the penetrability of matter are very ingenious, and not easily answered; but they do not equally affect the common hypothesis of the constituent particles of all bodies being prevented from actually touching one another by some power of repulsion, which however seems absolutely necessary to account for their condensation by cold, and dilation by heat?

Mr. Nichell supposes that wherever the properties or powers of any substance are, there is the substance itself, something that we may call *substance* being necessary to the support of any properties; but what any substance is, devoid of all properties, we cannot, from the nature of the thing, have any idea whatever; since all the notices that we receive of any substance are communicated to us by means of its properties, and such as bear some relation to our senses, which are the inlets to all our knowledge. And any property may be ascribed to any substance that does not necessarily imply a contradiction, that is, that does not suppose the absence of some other property.

Boscovich seems to suppose that matter consists of *powers* only, without any substance; but this differs from the theory of Berkeley, which excludes all space as well as matter.[12]

Priestley's formulations here are not exact. Matter existed for Boscovich, but as a dynamic configuration of a finite number of point-sources of mutual influences (which he later called centres of force); while space was for him much what it was for Leibniz, the order of existence of things possible at the same time.[13] But no doubt Priestley felt that he needed only broad statements for a man like Bretland.

We can trace the Boscovichian perspective in many of his comments. In 1793, in *Experiments on the Generation of Air from Water,* he wrote:

the advances we are continually making in the analyses of natural substances into the *elements* or which they consist, bring us but one step nearer to their constitutional differences; since as much depends upon the *mode of arrangement*, concerning which we know nothing at all, as upon the elements themselves. For things the most different in the properties appear to consist of the very same elements. Thus the nitrous acid, nitrous air, fixed air, phlogisticated air, alkaline air, and probably all the kinds of air with which we are acquainted, except the dephlogisticated and inflammable, are all composed of dephlogisticated air and phlogiston.[14]

Thus, in however abstracted a way, he was thinking in terms of a unitary system of matter with different structurations. As he was concerned here with inorganic matter, it is fair to say that he was anticipating molecular models. And this concept of his (of a single stream of matter differentiated by its inner structures) is bound up with Boscovichian atomism. The structures are determined, or built up, by systems of attraction and repulsion. In a letter to Wedgwood, 8 December 1782, he makes a particularly clear statement on this point. 'I had also a general idea that if the parts of any body be rarefied beyond the sphere of *attraction*, they will be in a sphere of repulsion to each other.'[15]

It is significant that Davy felt a sort of affinity with Priestley. He declared that the latter's books were those most likely to 'lead a student into the path of discovery'.[16] And he himself used Boscovichian ideas as a framework for research, taking up the notion of a specific property resulting from molecular form: the molecules being considered to consist of Boscovichian puncta. And Faraday in turn built on Davy, developing the idea of a chemical compound as the result of interlocking attractive forces.[17] Thus electro-chemistry in the hands of Davy and Faraday modified and redirected many Lavoisier positions – and precisely by concentrating on 'the principle, and the mode of combination' that Priestley stressed.[18]

Clearly, then, Priestley's opposition to Lavoisier was not simply the result of scientific weakness. His opposition derived from the fact that he had larger theories and issues in his mind which had become tied up with the phlogiston theory and which Lavoisier seemed to be ignoring or undermining.

The different 'states' in which the phlogiston, contained in *precipitate per se* and mercury, existed, may well be different spheres of attraction in the Boscovichian scheme. The '*aerial form*' lost by air in combination, which also goes to explain Priestley's frequent references to the loss of elasticity and the decrease of volume as significant parameters in his experiments. The 'different circumstances' or 'different methods of combining airs' and the possibility that airs behaved differently if united after or during the act of their formation, as they are 'dislodged' from the substances that yield them – which Priestley thought might explain the varying production of water or fixed air from inflammable or dephlogisticated airs, or the differences between his results and those of Berthollet – suggest physical mechanisms for molecule formation which are best understood in a Boscovichian frame. [SCHOFIELD][19]

We may glance at some of the statements in letters which illuminate these points. First, in a letter to Franklin, 24 June 1782:

Please too inform the Duc De Rochefocault, whose civilities to me I remember with pleasure, that my experiments are certainly inconsistent with Mr. Lavoisier's supposition, of there being no such thing as phlogiston, and that it is the addition of *air,* and not the loss of any thing that converts a metal into a calx. In their usual state calces of metals do contain air, but that may be expelled by heat; and after this I reduce them to a perfect metallic state by nothing but inflammable air, which they imbibe in toto, without any decomposition. I lately reduced 101 Ounce measures of this air to *two* by calx of lead, and that small remainder was still inflammable.
I explain Mr. Lavoisier's experiments by supposing that *precipitate per se* contains all the phlogiston of the metal mercury, but in a different state;

but I can shew other calces which also contain more phlogiston than the metals themselves. That mercury in its metallic state, does contain phlogiston, or inflammable air, is evident from the production of nitrous air by the solution of it in spirits of nitre, and I make *nitrous air* from nothing but *nitrous vapour* and *inflammable air* so that it indisputably consists of those two ingrediants.

I have already ascertained the proportion of inflammable air that enters into the composition of *lead, tin, copper,* and *silver,* and am proceeding to the other metals as fast as I can.[20]

Secondly, his reference to air as having its own particular form occurs in a letter to Wedgwood, 6 May 1783:

By means of Mr. Parker's lens, I heat an earthen retort, filled with moistened clay. When the neck of it is well luted to the upper orifice of a glass receiver, which is placed in a bason of water, and a glass tube communicates with the inside of the retort. In consequence of this, the water from the clay comes into the receiver, while the air in the receiver passes through the retort, and is delivered at a [thin end of retort]; the water in the bason rising within the receiver, and covering the retort. If it be inflammable air, it comes through inflammable, if nitrous, nitrous. This must be by the air losing its aerial form while it combines with the earth of the retort, and recovers its aerial form in the inside of it. If the retort was not perfectly air tight, the water could not rise within the receiver. Spirit of wine comes thro the retort into the receiver, just as the water does.[21]

Thirdly, for his ideas about 'different methods of combining airs' we may take a letter to W. Wilkinson, 16 June 1784:

A very interesting problem with us of late has been to determine what becomes of dephlogisticated and inflammable air, when they are made to unite, as by exploding then with the electric spark &c.; some saying that they make *water,* others *fixed air* &c. The following experiments show that, in different circumstances, they make *both:* and also that dephlogisticated air incorporates with *iron* in a great porportion. . . .

Another experiment that I have made shews a remarkable difference between inflammable air from *metals,* and that from *charcoal.* Having mixed a quantity of each of them with half as much dephlogisticated air, I exploded that from *iron,* by means of the electric spark, and found neither water nor fixed air; but firing the mixture that contained the inflammable air from *charcoal* (which shewed no sign of its containing any fixed air) $3\frac{1}{2}$ Ounce measures of the mixture yielded an evident quantity of water, and likewise almost an Ounce measure of pure fixed air. . . .[22]

To M. von Marum, 12 December 1788:

. . . I prove that when the inflammable and dephlogisticated airs are already formed, the decomposition of them produces the *nitrous acid*; but that if either of them unite with the other in the act of its formation, as it is dislodged from the substance that yields it, the produce, in all the cases which are very many, is uniformly *fixed air.* Water is clearly, in my opinion, an element in the composition of all kinds of air.[23]

There can then be no doubt that Boscovichian concepts had sunk deep into his thinking and conditioned much of his interpretation of experiments; but we can perhaps go further still in analysing his adherence to phlogiston and his resistance to Lavoisier's conclusions.

4 Phlogiston and Lavoisier

Critics of Priestley have often asserted that he was too haphazard in his experiments, too lacking in any clear sense of objectives, too vague in his understanding of the value of quantitative analysis; hence his inability to grasp what Lavoisier was doing. But it will be evident from what has already been said here that so far from being haphazard, he had a very definite underlying philosophy of matter and its changes, and that, though he shared his colleagues' shyness or disinclination to state plainly the theoretical views that led him to tackle various problems, he seems more than any of them to have been dominated by clear views on certain fundamental issues. 'I have of late been very busy about some experiments on *air*, with respect to respiration and vegetation, and flatter myself that I have discovered what I have long been in quest of,' he wrote to Lindsey on 23 August 1771, 'viz. that process in nature by which air, rendered noxious by breathing, is restored to its former salubrious condition.'[1] He speaks more freely in a letter; in a paper on the subject he would not have admitted that he had been carrying on a series of experiments with a definite aim in his mind. We must therefore take with a grain of salt his protestations to Fabroni (connected with the laboratory of the Grand Duke of Tuscany) about some experiments with willows and various airs: 'The facts appear to me to be rather extraordinary. You must help me to explain them, for I am a very bad theorist.' And again: 'My knowledge in chymistry is very imperfect, and I want such a guide as you would be.' He is being particularly polite to this foreigner, whom indeed he seems to have respected very much for his wide knowledge.[2]

In the *Memoirs* he stresses the way in which he forgot fields which he had once studied. In a letter of 13 April 1777 to Cappe he puts the same point, but links it with his capacity for extreme concentration on some particular theme for a period.

My manner has always been to give my whole attention to a subject till I have satisfied myself with respect to it, and then think no more about the matter. I hardly ever look into any thing that I have published; and when I do, it sometimes appears quite new to me.[3]

But he is making this deprecatory comment after an apology:

I am afraid you will think I have not taken so much pains to finish the Lectures [apparently those *On Oratory and Criticism*] as you could have wished; but I did as much as I well could, without studying the subject afresh, and I could not bring my mind to it, it is so long since I gave any attention to things of that nature.

He adds also that 'I have had more illness, and what I find to be a consequence of illness, more indolence, than usual for some time past; but I hope with care and exercise I shall get better in both respects.'

What seems true is that while more than any other of the chemists or physicists of the period he had a unifying scheme at the back of his thoughts, the gap between this scheme and the empirical methods he shared with the others made him wander in various directions and fail to make any consistent effort to link the experiments with the scheme. If he had been able to make that effort he would have been one of the greatest of scientists, would have been able to test and modify the scheme, and link the experiments steadily with a clarified world outlook. At this phase of science it would no doubt have been impossible to do all that – what we may call the gap between Boscovich and Lavoisier had to continue for a long time; indeed we cannot say that it has yet been effectively closed.

It was natural enough, then, that Priestley failed to see the importance of quantitative measurements. 'I have two more acid airs, the vitriolic and the vegetable, and also a species of air got from red lead, and other substances, that is near six times as good as common air' (to G. Walker, probably before 6 April 1775).[4] True, not till Lavoisier was the quantitative principle fully established, but there had been steps on the way, as for example in Joseph Black's work. Before 1720 Stephen Hales had invented a technique for collecting gases over water; Priestley substituted mercury when at work on water-soluble gases. Hales had investigated 'airs' produced by many processes, much interested in finding the quantity begotten by a given weight of materials, but he drew no new qualitative distinctions between the different airs; he only concluded that air could be fixed in substances as a solid. Joseph Black at last definitely placed such a fixed air as well as demonstrating its function in several reactions. Rough identifications of airs was not new (*e.g.* flame-extinguishing, or inflammable), but none of them had been clearly distinguished from common air or allotted a specific function in chemical processes. Black, in his *Experiments upon Magnesia alba*, 1756, showed a definite quantitative relationship in his proof that quicklime was limestone deprived of fixed-air; and he insisted that fixed-air was not identical with common-air. All his masterly demonstration was made without a mention of phlogiston.[5]

In 1756, however, the technique of collecting fugitive airs or 'elastic fluids' in vessels was still almost beyond the powers of chemists. Cavendish in *Three Papers concerning Experiments on Factitious Airs*, 1766, described it. In his first paper he distinguished between Black's fixed-air and another (hydrogen) which he found lighter than common-air and thought to be derived from metals. About the same time the Swedish apothecary C. W. Scheele separated the two major components of the atmosphere (*Feuerluft*, oxygen, and *verdorbene Luft*, nitrogen), and prepared oxygen in various ways, as did Priestley independently. With Cavendish, Scheele, Priestley, the analysis was made in phlogistic terms, though Cavendish called oxygen dephlogisticated water and Priestley dephlogisticated air. The decisive step, however, was taken by Lavoisier's insistence on weight as the most important parameter in chemical change.

We may lay it down as an incontestable axiom, that, in all the operations of art and nature, nothing is created; an equal quantity of matter exists both before and after the experiment; the quality and quantity of the elements remain precisely the same; and nothing takes place beyond changes and modifications in the combination of these elements.[6]

Without entering into the controversial details we may claim that Priestley's conversation of October 1774 with Lavoisier and his following experiments (which established that his dephlogisticated air was respirable as well as able to support combustion) led on to Lavoisier's announcement in August 1778 that the air, combined with a metal, formed a calx, and, combined with charcoal, produced Black's fixed-air (carbon dioxide). Again it was work of Cavendish in 1782 (carrying on experiments begun by Priestley and others with an electric spark) that showed hydrogen and oxygen fusing in the ratio 2:1 to produce water. By June 1783 Lavoisier heard of these results and, with little acknowledgment of Cavendish, incorporated them in his thesis. Finally, in 1787, with three adherents, he devised the new nomenclature, still substantially used, of oxygen, hydrogen, and so on.

Incidentally, the emphasis on weight was the only part of his oxidation theory that survived unscathed.[7]

At this point it would be as well to look in more detail at the phlogistic theory, which had been set out by the German chemist G. E. Stahl (1660–1734) on principles largely taken from J. J. Becher (whose *Physicae Subterranae* he republished in 1703). We may describe Stahl's ideas as the last form taken by the alchemic tradition, or perhaps rather as the transitional stage between alchemy and modern chemistry. His principles were water and three earths (corresponding to the three principles of the iatrochemists); he did not see air as chemically active. The second earth (sulphur) he called phlogiston. Stahl's followers, who multiplied after 1730, made much use of the notion of affinity in explaining reactions; and though phlogiston was by no means the sole feature of their chemical creed, it had a central place through its use as a co-ordinating factor; and it was this use, which seemed to link and explain many previously isolated data, which gave the theory its historical place as the necessary prelude to chemistry proper.[8] Phlogiston, we noted above, was thought to be a substance emitted during combustion, and the theory saddled chemists with a problem of weight: where a modern chemist sees a gain or loss of oxygen, the phlogistic exponent saw an inverse loss or gain of phlogiston. Oxygen has weight; a chemist would declare that phlogiston should have negative weight – and indeed an argument along those lines was put out in the dying days of Stahl's theory. But before gases were collected and the gain or loss of weight due to the part played by a gaseous element in a chemical reaction measured, the question of phlogistic weights could not engross men's minds. Watson in *Chemical Essays*, 1782, could declare:

You do not surely expect that chemistry should be able to present you with a handful of phlogiston, separated from an inflammable body; you may as reasonably demand a handful of magnetism, gravity, or electricity. . . . There are powers in nature which cannot otherwise become the objects of sense, than by the effects they produce; and of this kind is phlogiston.[9]

The plea was already beginning to lose its persuasiveness; but not till the impact of Lavoisier's work was felt would its validity have been questioned by most thinkers. Priestley would have agreed with it till the end. Indeed he wrote in 1796:

The phlogiston theory is not without its difficulties. The chief of them is that we are not able to ascertain the *weight* of phlogiston, or indeed that of the oxygenous principle. But neither do any of us pretend that we have weighed *light*, or the element of *heat*, though we do not doubt that they are properly *substances*, capable by their addition or abstraction, of making great changes in the properties of bodies, and of being transmitted from one substance to another.[10]

He is aware of the importance being attached to weight, but evades the fact that oxygen was being weighed. However what matters to us here are the terms which he and Watson used, and which help us to understand why he clung to the phlogiston theory. He wanted a principle of chemical action as striking and as universal as were those of gravitation, magnetism and electricity in their own spheres. Some scholars have suggested that chemists had in effect identified phlogiston with energy, and Robert Mayer, one of the founders of the modern mechanical theory of heat, held this opinion.[11] Again, it has been proposed that the seventeenth-century chemists meant by phlogiston the potential energy of the combustible substance – or more exactly, of the combustible substance plus oxygen.

It is only when these two unite that this energy is transformed into a kinetic.... No compound contains the substances from which it is produced but it contains then *minus* something. [CRUM BROWN][12]

Clearly we cannot accept these suggestions if they mean that the phlogiston theorists held the modern ideas of energy in any precise sense; but they do, correctly enough, point to an undefined conception, larger than anything in the stated theory, which haunted the minds of its important exponents. Priestley in particular felt in the theory certain comprehensive elements, leading in his view to vast simplifications and interconnections in the whole scientific field; and it was the potentiality of the phlogiston outlook which he felt jeopardised by Lavoisier's formulations.

As he struggled to combat Lavoisier, he was forced to grapple more than he had done with theory; but he could do this as adequately as he wanted to. In his later lectures at Hackney he linked gravitational attractions, cohesion, and chemical affinity.[13] So, interestingly, we see Priestley, who in so many ways has appeared as a mechanist, violently resisting mechanist theory in Lavoisier's quantitative form and struggling for a much more complex understanding of the nature of energy, of attraction-and-repulsion, and of cohesive stabilities or symmetries. Lavoisier's position assumed Newtonian action-at-a-distance, and it was because of this fact that it so quickly won over the French mathematical scientists who were trying to build up an axiomatic Newtonian mechanics. Phlogistonists could in reply take the line of denying the fundamental nature of gravity as a property of matter; they turned instead to the variant Newtonian concept of the Aether – for example James Hutton in Scotland and Gren in Germany.[14]

Priestley, however, accepted action-at-a-distance, yet did not accept the onsequences as to weight (or mass).

To Boscovich gravitational mass was quantity derived from the near identity of his attractive at sensible distances to the inverse-square law of Newton, and he declares that '. . . the idea of mass is not strictly definite and distinct, but. . . is quite vague, arbitrary and confused'. Priestley not only adopted this view, he also denies inertial mass to have meaning, when he insists that matter is not sluggish, inert, or possessed of vis inertiæ, though Newton's laws of motion were still valid within the Boscovich theory. That he extends this belief into his scientific work is suggested by Priestley's consistent failure to use mass as a significant and operative parameter in his own work and by the ineptness and illogic he displays in trying to meet Lavoisier's weight observations with his own. . . . Priestley might well have argued that mass derived from the effects of a sphere of attraction binding particles at less than sensible distances would be a different thing entirely from gravitational mass and could hardly be regarded as a fixed parameter for all distances from a material point, with its varying spheres of attraction and repulsion.[15]

Here we seem to touch the heart of the matter. Priestley, with his fusion of Newtonian, Hartleian and Boscovichian principles, was intuiting issues which have only come home to us of recent years and which are still far from anything like an adequate statement and solution. Boscovich's essential contribution has been defined as:

the building up of a *qualitative scheme for representing mechanical as well as other physical properties of matter* leading to a completely new view of the composition of matter. The emphasis is not on a special system of forces which represents or 'explains' the observed phenomena more or less well, but on the immense possibilities of variation and differentiation in the application of the scheme. [WHYTE][16]

Hence its attractions for Faraday, its use by Kelvin, and the way in which its idea of a curve-of-forces served J. J. Thomson, who created the theory of electrons, in developing the first concepts of the new atomic physics. It will also serve the thinker who is able to bring decisive order into that physics (and other scientific fields) by finding the 'single law' that Boscovich and Priestley both desired so ardently.

Priestley's clinging to phlogiston, then, in the last resort, does not show an archaic viewpoint but on the contrary reveals an intuition of problems and solutions that looked far beyond Lavoisier. His breadth of view blinded him, however, to the lesser issue which held the clue to progress after 1775. And this conclusion may drive us to look back and ask if after all his mechanism is quite so mechanical as it is easy to assume. True, he could not effectively define the relation of free will and necessity, of external circumstances and inner movement, in terms of a materialist philosophy – a failure, if we are so to call it, which he shares with a distinguished company. The contradictions which we noted that he carried on from Hartley derived from this fact. He used the Christian idiom and clung to a firm faith in the Gospels (stripped bare of all 'superstition' and 'idolatry') perhaps because he could find no other way of transcending the mechanist elements in his social, scientific and psychological theories and of emotionally resolving the contradictions. He had no concept of a hierarchy of levels or of forms of development, except in what we may call the ghost-dialectic haunting the interstices of the contradictions and providing the dynamic for his sense of a great joyous drive on into new dimensions of knowledge and experience. In the fuller perspective which we are now able to take we may claim that he accepted the mechanistic advances of post-Galilean science as a necessary basis for any full grasp of reality: or rather, as the historically provided and conditioned springboard for any advance in his world into a unitary conception of mind and matter. Inevitably he could not fully compass that conception. His intuition of unitary process was continually defeated and driven back into partial or mechanistically-limited accounts of what happens in natural or historical process. But once we get beneath the limitations, the fragmentary insights or discoveries, we touch on the deep feeling he had for the unity of life, of man and nature, of mind and matter, and the conviction he thus gained of man, organically involved with the total scheme of things, moving steadily on to a 'perfectibility' which stably expressed his coming-of-age as a species, his true discovery and creation of the universe as his home. All this, rather than any particular achievement, is what constitutes the lasting interest of Priestley as man and thinker. As one enters into his mind and character, one feels that he deserves the fine summing-up of Toplady: 'I love a man whom I can hold up as a piece of crystal, and look through him. For this I have always admired Dr. Priestley.'[17]

NOTES TO INTRODUCTION

1 *Joseph Priestley*

1. Rutt, Holt, Gibb, Thorpe, and Schofield (1) hereafter referred to as SA.
2. Timothy P., 42 f.
3. SA 3.
4. J. W. A. Smith, 131; Gow. 's Gravesande visited England as secretary to an embassy, 1715, when he came to know Newton and was made F.R.S.; in 1734, professor of philosophy at Leyden; he died 1742.
5. J. Williams, 224–6; SA 5; Gibb 17 f.
6. SA 7; Gibb 21, 34. For Daventry, Belsham, *Mem. Lindsey* (1812) 286.
7. Gibb 21; *The Works of A. L. Barbauld,* 1825, 29, 46; Rutt i 46, 49, 54, 60, 282, 285, 288, 362; ii 57, 367, 411: the last two pages for her poem to Mrs. P. and his letter 23 Dec. 1798: 'You have obliged me very much by the exquisite little poem you sent me. I hope you will add to my obligation by the communication of the fragment on the game of Chess, or any other little pieces you may think proper to send me. You had no copy of your first poem to my wife, or I should value *that* above any other; and also the little poem you wrote on the birth of Joseph.' For his attitude to Sunday, Rutt i 17.
8. For letters of this period: *Christian Reformer,* 1854, × n.s. 625 ff.; for the Academy, Gibb pl. 4. Simpson's account: Rutt i 50 f.
9. *Phil. Emp.,* 1775, 45. Turner was a Republican; in a debating society at Liverpool, near the end of the American war, he remarked (when one speaker descanted on the honour gained by Britain under George's reign) that 'it was true we had lost the *terra firma* of the thirteen colonies in America, but we ought to be satisfied with having gained in return, by the generality of Dr. Herschel, a *terra incognita* of much greater extent *in nubibus*'. He is said to have invented or perfected that art of copying prints on glass 'by baking on an iron plate in a heat sufficient to incorporate the solution with the glass', Rutt i 76.
10. SA 10; Gibb 52, 72, 161 f. Gibb 12 for possible early effect of W. Brownrigg's *The Art of Making Common Salt,* 1748, with preface on relation of 'mechanic arts' to a true science of nature. Note in general the links of industrial chemistry with the new impulse given to chemical studies. In France the theory of manufacturing processes was explored by men like Réaumur, Macquer, Duhamel du Monceau: in England chemical science helped to bring about new industries.
11. We may note the link of explosive or destructive force between electricity (thunderbolt) and gases etc. I hope elsewhere to trace the connection of science in the bourgeois epoch with artillery (ballistics and explosive forces) leading finally to nuclear fission, jet propulsion etc. There is a psychological unity in all this, a deep unconscious obsession that has yet to be overcome and resolved in a new kind of science with a completely new perspective on energy.
12. Aepinus, etc., Hall 355 f.: also for more on Cavendish's quantitative work. The French engineer Coulomb also verified the theorem. See further Berry 92 ff. Letter to Canton: SA no 10.
13. *Hist. of Present State of Elec.,* 1767, p. xiii; also 502 f.; Schofield (8) 168.
14. Gill 44 f.; SA no 17a.
15. SA no 120. More on photosynthesis: Rutt i 148 ff.
16. Rutt i 331 f.
17. SA 136.

18. Holt 94 (*Early Life of S. Rogers*, 266); Willey 165. The *Journal* (given in the *Memoirs*) is from Rutt ii 237–51. See also letters: 251–5.

19. He also made experiments in sound and heating-by-compression; worked on fluor acide air (silicon fluoride); went on all the while with electrical experiments. In 1774 he sold the telescope with which he began to study optics; but in 1777 collaborated with J. Waltire in trying to measure refractive indices of gases; in 1780 got optical information for Herschel. Five telescopes of his were destroyed at Birmingham, including a refractor with 14-foot focus.

20. Berry 118 f.

21. SA no 79.

22. SA no 80.

23. Rutt i 274 f.

24. SA no 129

25. Gales was later in America. Writing to Lindsey, 11 Sept. 1796, Priestley said, 'I do not know that I have had more satisfaction from any thing I ever did, than from the lay Unitarian congregation I have been the means of establishing in Philadelphia. Mr. Gales (who was a printer in Sheffield) writes me word, that they increase, and that all who attend have increasing satisfaction in it' (Rutt ii 352). Gales in England: G. A. Williams, 59–61, 66, 103.

26. The exact role played by Priestley, Cavendish, Watt, and Lavoisier in the discovery of water's composition has been much debated, and can only be dealt with by detailed analyses. In any event it was Lavoisier who gave the crucial explanation, and Priestley threw all the weight of his name into combating it. See SA 268–70; Berry ch. 4; Muirhead; Wilson; Edelstein; Schofield (5).

27. SA no. 134.

28. Gibb 197 f.

29. Randell 65 f.

30. Rutt ii 152; for other letters 126 ff.

31. He recalled Hackney in exile as well as the Lunar Society: 22 March 1795, to Rev. T. Belsham, '. . . your success in the congregation, and in your lectures to my class at Hackney'. And 3 Aug. 1795, 'What I want chiefly is the *employment* I had at Hackney . . .' (Rutt ii 397, 313).
Priestley left England in fact just in time. 1795–6 saw the fall of the English Jacobins. Some stopped agitation; some went to France; hardship drove thousands into the army and made the government uncomfortably aware of Jacobins in the ranks – there were some 15,000 Irish in the navy at the time of the mutinies. The emigration to America was considerable, with its peak 1795–1800. The Federalists there hated them, and the Alien and Sedition Acts were directed against them as much as against the Irish; they were active in the liberty-settlements.

32. SA no 152.

33. SA 326 f.; Rutt ii 485 f.; L. P. Williams 160 (on Hutton's defence of phlogiston). An important use of Boscovich was made by J. Thomson in a *A System of Chemistry*, 4 vols., 1802.

34. SA no 152.

35. Rutt ii 487: he here mentions that 'unbelievers in revelation' at times 'lean, as many of them do, to that doctrine' – an example of the link of scientific and religious or anti-religious ideas. Note his horror at meeting such doctrines in France, Rutt i 254 f. See further, Abrahams.

36. In these last years he seems to have revived his pleasure in direct contemplation of Nature. To Lindsey, 26 June 1802 (Rutt ii 487): 'Whether it be, because I converse less with *men*, in this remote situation, I contemplate the scenes of *nature*, as the production of its great Author, more, and with more satisfaction, than I

ever did before; and the new discoveries that are now making in every branch of science, interest me more than ever in this connexion. I see before us a boundless field of the noblest investigation. . . . I now take great pleasure in garden. . . . I wish I knew a little more of botany; but, old as I am, I learn something new continually.'

2 *Priestley and Hartley*

1. He favoured Mrs. Stephens' cure, which largely consisted of soap; and he is said to have consumed some 200 lb. before he died: Gentlemen's Mag. May 1746. Among poems he admired was Hawkins Browne's *De Anime Immortalitate*.
2. *Life*, in 1801 ed. (based on Pistorius, 3 vols.); despite Priestley, Hartley seems rather ignored till about 1791.
3. Newton, *Principia*, Motte's transl. 1729 (ed. Cajoli 1934), preface to first edition; cf. *Opticks* iii pt. i qu. 31 (1704: reprint E. T. Whittaker, 1931); Willey 135 f.
4. 1801, i 500; 'prescience' 510.
5. Gay, *Dissertation* sect. iv.
6. *Obs.* propositions i, ii and ix, x. Vibratiuncles, xiii, xiv.
7. *Obs.* i 111 (1749).
8. His son (1801, ii p. ix) notes, 'It was from the union of talents in the moral sciences with natural philosophy, and particularly from the professional knowledge of the human frame, that Dr. Hartley was enabled to bring into one view the various argument for his extensive system, from the first rudiments of sensation through the maze of complex affections and passions in the path of life, to the final, moral end of man.'
9. 1749, i 82 f., 368.
10. *Ib.* 81.
11. See Willey 141; I should like to follow further these interesting points. Wordsworth, *Letter to 'The Friend'*, Dec. 1809–Jan. 1810.
12. *Obs.* 1749, ii 214.
13. 1801, i 493.
14. *Ib.* ii 254; 1749 i 431–42 and ii 244–54. See Willey 142 on Imagination.
15. 1801, i 419.
16. *Ib.* i 324.
17. *Ib.* ii 441.
18. *Hist. of Corruptions of Christianity* (Works, Rutt v 4); Willey 164.
19. Gibb 195 f.
20. Rutt ii 245. For the early poem, i 19. At Warrington, 7 Jan. 1767 (Rutt i 67): 'Newberry's little pieces are sufficient for English reading before boys can read the Spectator; or give them "The Animal World Displayed", an excellent book for young persons; Newberry's "Voyages and Travels", which will be useful in studying geography; and at leisure hours let them read Robinson Crusoe. I had a kind of school library of such books, and there is no better exercise for young persons than after reading a story to them distinctly, to require an account of it in writing.'
6 Dec. 1795: 'I have just seen Mr. Fawcett's Poem on War, in a copy sent to Mr. Cooper, from Mr. Hawkes, of Manchester. It discovers a most exuberant imagination, but so many words and phrases for one idea, I never saw before. Some parts are very affecting.' The poem was *The Art of War*.
1 Nov. 1798: 'Mr. Scott, my neighbour at Ipswich, when I was at Needham, in Suffolk, published a poetical version of the book of Job, with large critical notes.

I lost it in the riots, and forgot to replace it.' For Mrs. Barbauld, note I, 7. He seems much interested in Petrarch: Rutt i 418; ii 426, 480, 353.

For the importance of the Latin expository poem from the sixteenth century on (note Buchanan read on the boat), cf. Bruno's poems, the poem by Benedict Stay (for which Boscovich wrote notes (3 vols. 1755, 1760, 1792); Boscovich's *Eclipses* (done into French by Abbé de Barnel 1779), etc.

21. Willey 165.
22. *Disquisitions*, 1777, 109; Willey 168. Immortality, *Disq.* 156; soul, 31.
23. *Disq.* 222.
24. Hartley *Obs.* i 497 f. (1749). For doctrine of Law on the 'Keep of the soul', Rutt i 23.
25. Rutt i 315. Calvinist gloom: i 12 and 259.
26. Willey 186 ff.
27. *Ib.* 188 f. See also Rutt i 53.
28. See for ex. Bower; Gibb 34, 95-7, 216 f., 250; Rutt i 52, etc. Note that near the end P. read and admired Malthus: Rutt ii 325.
29. *Lectures*, 1788, progress 532; against the notion of a past Golden Age 324.
30. Rutt i 146. Lindsey sees history as determined by God, but man plays his part when he co-operates with God and struggles for perfectibility. 'Our cause will prosper now, if we fall in with the plan of Divine government . . .' (Rutt i 147).
31. Rutt ii 315.
32. Rutt ii 410.
33. Rutt ii 127-30.
34. Rutt ii 190 f.
35. SA no 153. For Kirwan: SA 207, 211, 214, 220, 225, 227 f., 290, 324; Rutt ii 2, 431, 470.

For his sympathy with Muir and Palmer, Rutt ii 325 (cf. 221, 226; for many refs. to Palmer, see index Rutt. He shows no sympathy for Toussaint l'Ouverture, ii 477, taking him for a mere adventurer; probably he was still so much a partisan of the French that he saw only their side. He continues to seek the explanation of revolutionary change in Prophecy *e.g.* ii 289 f., and 312 on Richard Brothers. On 19 Feb. 1802 (Rutt ii 472-6) the lull in hostilities revived his hopes of communications with France; no doubt it was a blow to him that the revolutionary land in which he put such high hopes should turn from his theories. 'As to my visiting Europe, it is now too late in life to think of it, and my health has received a rude shock by a fever I had at Philadelphia. . . . Were I younger, and could speak French fluently, I should not hesitate about it. . . . Could I be persuaded that any good could arise to rational Christianity by my removing to France, I should not hesistate about it. . . .' Note that it is France, not England, that tempts him to make a return.

By October he felt saddened. The imperial developments in France at last upset him as nothing done during the revolutionary period had. 'All the friends of liberty must have been disappointed with respect to France' (Rutt ii 497).

His direct influence appeared most strongly in the works and ideas of Bentham and Mill; but as this seems to me the more arid side of his work I have not tried here to trace it, or to deal with the later developments of the Association Theory, in which many important and interesting aspects appear (from 1790 on). I have glanced at the effect of the Hartley–Priestley tradition on Wordsworth, and much more might be said in that relation. I have not dealt with his impact on Coleridge or with the well-known tale of Coleridge, Southey, and Pantisocracy, the utopian hopes roused by the Revolution and the migrations to America, and the part played by T. Cooper and Priestley's son. We may note, however, Coleridge's letter to Southey, 6 Sept. 1794, and his verse-tributes, the sonnet and *Religious Musings*, Dec. 1794: Willey 185; L. Hanson, *Life of S.T.C.*, 1938, 52; Rutt ii 232; Gibb 326 f. etc. etc. I cite instead a poem by the Rev. Edward Garnham, close friend of Lindsey (Rutt ii 232):

> *March 4, 1794, recovering from gout.*
> The savage, slavish Britain now no more
> Deserves this patriot's steps to print her shore.
> Despots and leagues and armies overthrown,
> France would exult to claim him as her own.
> Yet no! America, whose soul aspires
> To warm her sons with Europe's brightest fires;
> Whose virtue, science, scorns a second prize,
> Asks and obtains our Priestley from the skies.
> Ye storms, ye monsters, which the seas contain,
> Let him uninjured cross a placid main;
> For never did your gentler breasts engage
> Passions so fell as sacerdotal rage.

36. John Gage, *Colour in Turner* (1969) 130 f., also citing E. Darwin; and 255 n 14 for sea-phorescence in the 1799 Naumachia; 256 n 18 for pearly fish in *Calais Pier*. Notes in Goethe, p. 256.

3 Boscovich and Priestley

1. This is the formulation of L. L. Whyte.
2. Markovič 131.
3. *Ib.* 132.
4. The *puncta* are all identical; it is not clear if he thought they could be identified in physical systems. In a way the concept goes back to the Pythagoreans, who represented numbers by dot-patterns; but the naïve picture of hard atoms was not overcome till Rutherford. Boscovich also carried on the Pythagorean spirit in his dream of a universe of fundamental structure, though he extended the law to cover all motions under a generalised super-Newtonian law.
5. For Vico's notion of points: Whyte 118; Swedenborg also published in 1734 a doctrine of material points, with a tendency to motion, as the source of all geometrical phenomena. There is thus a sequence: Vico, Leibniz, Swedenborg, Boscovich, Michell, Kant: Whyte 119.
6. Whyte 119.
7. I. P. Williams 154.
8. *Hist. . . . of Disc. rel. to Vision*, 1772, 198, 308, 383, 392; A. Geikie 76–83.
9. Whyte 168 f.
10. Opticks 177, 393; also 308, 390–4. Cavendish never mentioned Boscovich though we may assume he knew his work; he probably met him. Birch, Sec. of the Royal Society, noted, 'June 26. 1760. Dined in the Mitre with the Earl of Macclesfield, Lord Cha. Cavendish, Dr. Bradley, Father Boscovich.' Lord Charles was Henry C.'s father.
11. D. Hill 64 f.
12. Rutt i 189 f.
13. Markovič 144; Whyte 117.
14. *Experiments* 38; SA 274 (for all these points).
15. SA no 100.
16. Davy vii 117.

17. L. P. Williams 160 ff., SA 328.
18. Priestley, *New York Medical Repository* v 1802, 266: 'Indeed, a knowledge of the *elements* which enter into the composition of natural substances, is but a small part of what is desirable to investigate with respect to them, the principle, and the mode of their combination; as how it is that they become hard or soft, elastic or non-elastic, solid or fluid, &c. &c. &c. is quite another subject, of which we have, as yet, very little knowledge, or rather none at all.' SA 327.
19 SA 274.
20. SA no 95.
21. SA no 111, cf. letter to J. Watt, 29 April 1783, in Bolton no 25.
22. SA no 119; Bolton no 31 makes it to John W.
23. SA no 133, cf. no 137 to Wedgwood Feb. 1791.

4 *Phlogiston and Lavoisier*

1. Rutt i 144–7; SA 133. Cf. 'random experiment', Berry 69.
2. SA nos 81 and 86 (20 June 1779 and 17 Oct.).
3. Rutt i 298 f.
4. SA no 63.
5. Hall 331 f.; Berry 39 f. Black said, 'to this I have given the name *fixed air*, and perhaps very improperly; but I thought it better to use a word already familiar in philosophy, than to invent a new name'. G. Wilson remarks that 'the word gas had no certain plural till his (Black's) time, and Cavendish was his acknowledged pupil'.
6. Berry 47 f.
7. *Elements of Chemistry*, transl. R. Kerr, 1790, 130; also Hall 334–40.
In the *Traité Elémentaire de Chimie* Lavoisier set down his new attitude thus: 'All that can be said about the number and nature of elements seems to me to be discussions which are purely metaphysical, to be indeterminate problems capable of an infinite number of solutions, not one of which in all probability is consistent with nature. I shall, therefore, content myself with saying that if by the term elements we mean to express the simple and indivisible molecules that compose bodies, it is probable that we know nothing about them; but if, on the contrary, we express by the term elements or principles of bodies the idea of the last point reached by analysis, all substances that we have not been able to decompose by any means are elements to us.' (*Oeuvres complètes* i 7, 1864–9, 6 vols.)
Schofield remarks that P. fails to think in terms of composition and decomposition; he sees gases as 'released' from materials or contained in them. SA 194, 151, and no 64. In photosynthesis his plants do not transform one gas into another; air is concentrated in the green matter and disengaged by light: SA 194, 172, no 81. (For Scheele, SA 194: 'The object and chief business of chemistry (is) skilfully to separate substances into their constituents, to discover their properties, and to compound them in different ways,' A. Wolf 358.) But P. did use the term 'decomposed', *e.g.* SA nos 131–2; 'convert', no 104 (pure water into permanent air) and nos 101–3; 'convertible', no 105. Also no 104 has charcoal 'resolved' into its weight of inflammable air'. It seems, then, that his concept was not fixed, but wavered between a mechanistic idea of extraction and an alchemic one of conversion or resolution.
8. See Metzger for full analysis.
9. Watson i 167; Hall 329 f.
10. *Considerations on the Doctrine of Phlogiston, and the Decomposition of Water,* 1796, 59.
C

11. Helm, *Die Energetik nach ihrer historische Entwicklung*.
12. Berry 37 f.
13. *Heads of Lectures*, 1794, 12, cf. 4 f., 9–12, 149, 153.
14. J. R. Partington and D. Mckie (1) 8 and (2) 366; Schofield (8) 171.
15. Schofield (8) 171. Priestley, *Disq*. 353. Cavendish (*Philos. Trans*. lxi, 1771, 584–677), dealing with 'electric fluid', said that 'in all probability' its weight 'in any body bears but a very small proportion to the weight of the matter; but yet the force with which the electric fluid therein attracts any particle of matter must be equal to the force with which the matter therein repels that particle; otherwise the body would appear electrical, as will be shewn hereafter'. Maxwell pointed out that the comment on 'the weight of the electric fluid' as a measurable quantity implied what Boscovich and modern writers would express by the term *mass*: Berry 93.
16. Whyte 148.
17. Cited Rutt i 32. The only unamiable moment in his life that I can find is his blinding a dog in an electrical experiment, without a word of regret in his record of the event.

Memoirs written by Himself

Memoirs of Dr. Joseph Priestley
(written by himself)
with a Journal of his Travels

Having thought it right to leave behind me some account of my *friends* and *benefactors*, it is in a manner necessary that I also give some account of *myself*; and as the like has been done by many persons, and for reasons which posterity has approved, I make no further apology for following their example. If my writings in general have been useful to my contemporaries, I hope that this account of myself will not be without its use to those who may come after me, and especially in promoting virtue and piety, which, I hope I may say, it has been my care to practise myself, as it has been my business to inculcate them upon others.

My father, Jonas Priestley, was the youngest son of Joseph Priestley, a maker and dresser of woollen cloth. His first wife, my mother, was the only child of Joseph Swift, a farmer at Shafton, a village about six miles south-east of Wakefield. By this wife he had six children, four sons and two daughters. I, the oldest, was born on the thirteenth of March, old style, 1733, at Fieldhead, about six miles south-west of Leeds, in Yorkshire. My mother dying in 1740, my father married again in 1745, and by his second wife had three daughters.

My mother having children so fast, I was very soon committed to the care of her father, and with him I continued with little interruption till my mother's death.

It is but little that I can recollect of my mother. I remember, however, that she was careful to teach me the Assembly's Catechism, and to give me the best instructions the little time that I was at home. Once in particular, when I was playing with a pin, she asked me where I got it; and on telling her that I found it my uncle's, who lived very near to my father, and where I had been playing with my cousins, she made me carry it back again; no doubt to impress my mind, as it could not fail to do, with a clear idea of the distinction of property, and of the importance of attending to it. She died in the hard winter of 1739, not long after being delivered of my youngest brother; and having dreamed, a little before her death that she was in a delightful place, which she particularly described, and imagined to be heaven, the last words which she spake, as my aunt informed me, were 'let me go to that fine place'.

On the death of my mother I was taken home, my brothers taking my place, and was sent to school in the neighbourhood. But being without a mother, and my father incumbered with a large family, a sister of my father's, in the year 1742, relieved him of all care of me, by taking me entirely to herself, and considering me as her own child, having none of her own. From this time she was truly a parent to me, till her death in 1764.

My aunt was married to a Mr. Keighly, a man who had distinguished himself for his zeal for religion and for his public spirit. He was also a man of considerable property, and dying soon after I went to them, left the greatest part of his fortune to my aunt for life, and much of it at her disposal after her death.

By this truly pious and excellent woman, who knew no other use of wealth, or of talents of any kind, than to do good, and who never spared herself for this purpose, I was sent to several schools in the neighbourhood, especially to a large free school, under the care of a clergyman, Mr. Hague, under whom, at the age of twelve or thirteen, I first began to make any progress in the latin tongue, and acquired the elements of Greek. But about the same time that I began to learn Greek at this public school, I learned Hebrew on holidays of the dissenting minister of the place, Mr. Kirkby; and upon the removal of Mr. Hague from the free school, Mr. Kirkby opening a school of his own, I was wholly under his care. With this instruction, I had acquired a pretty good knowledge of the learned languages at the age of sixteen. But from this time, Mr. Kirkby's increasing infirmities obliged him to relinquish the school, and beginning to be of a weakly consumptive habit, so that it was not thought advisable to send me to any other place of education, I was left to conduct my studies as well as I could, till I went to the academy at Daventry, in the year 1752.

From the time I discovered any fondness for books, my aunt entertained hopes of my being a minister, and I readily entered into her views. But my ill health obliged me to turn my thoughts another way, and, with a view to trade, I learned the modern languages, French, Italian, and High Dutch, without a master; and in the first and last of them I translated and wrote letters, for an uncle of mine who was a merchant, and who intended to put me into a counting-house in Lisbon. A house was actually engaged to receive me there, and everything was nearly ready for my undertaking the voyage. But getting better health, my former destination for the ministry was resumed, and I was sent to Daventry, to study under Mr. Ashworth, afterwards Dr. Ashworth.

Looking back, as I often do, upon this period of my life, I see the greatest reason to be thankful to God for the pious care of my parents and friends, in giving me religious instruction. My mother was a woman of exemplary piety, and my father also had a strong sense of religion, praying with his family, morning and evening, and carefully teaching the children and servants the Assembly's Catechism, which was all the system of which he had any knowledge. In the latter part of his life, he became very fond of Mr. Whitfield's writings, and other works of a similar kind, having been brought up in the principles of Calvinism, and adopting them, but without ever giving much attention to matters of speculation, and entertaining no bigotted aversion to those who differed from him on the subject.

The same was the case with my excellent aunt, she was truly Calvinistic in principle, but was far from confining salvation to those who thought as she did on religious subjects. Being left in good circumstances, her home was the resort of all the dissenting ministers in the neighbourhood without distinction, and those who were the most obnoxious on account of their heresy were almost as welcome to her, if she thought them honest and good men (which she was not unwilling to do), as any others.

The most heretical ministers in the neighbourhood were Mr. Graham, of Halifax, and Mr. Walker, of Leeds; but they were frequently my aunt's guests. With the former of these, my intimacy grew with my years, but chiefly after I became a preacher. We kept up a correspondence to the last, thinking alike on most subjects. To him I dedicated my 'Disquisitions on Matter and Spirit', and when he died, he left me his manuscripts, his Polyglot Bible, and two hundred pounds. Besides being a rational Christian, he was an excellent classical scholar, and wrote Latin with great facility and elegance. He frequently wrote to me in that language.

Thus I was brought up with sentiments of piety, but without bigotry, and having, from my earliest years, given much attention to the subject of religion, I was as much confirmed as I well could be in the principles of Calvinism, all the books that came in my way having that tendency.

The weakness of my constitution, which often led me to think that I should not be long-lived, contributed to give my mind a still more serious turn; and having read many books of *experiences*, and, in consequence, believing that a *new birth*, produced by the immediate agency of the Spirit of God, was necessary to salvation, and not being able to satisfy myself that I *had* experienced any thing of the kind, I felt occasionally such distress of mind as it is not in my power to describe, and which I still look back upon with horror. Notwithstanding that I had nothing very material to reproach myself with, I often concluded that God had forsaken me, and that mine was like the case of Francis Spira, to whom, as he imagined, repentance and salvation were denied. In that state of mind, I remember reading the account of the man in the iron cage, in the 'Pilgrim's Progress', with the greatest perturbation.

I imagine that even these conflicts of mind were not without their use, as they led me to think habitually of God and a future state. And though my feelings were then, no doubt, too full of terror, what remained of them was a deep reverence for divine things, and in time a pleasing satisfaction which can never be effaced, and, I hope, was strengthened as I have advanced in life, and acquired more rational notions of religion. The remembrance, however, of what I sometimes felt in that state of the value of rational principles of religion, and of which I can give but an imperfect description to others.

As *truth*, we cannot doubt, must have an advantage over *error*, we may conclude that the want of these peculiar feelings is compensated by something of greater value, which arises to others from always having seen things in a just and pleasing light; from having always considered the Supreme Being as the kind parent of all his offspring. This, however, not having been my case, I cannot be so good a judge of the effects of it. At all events, we ought always to inculcate just views of things, assuring ourselves that *proper feelings and right conduct* will be the consequence of them.

In the latter part of the interval between my leaving the grammar-school and going to the academy, which was something more than two years, I attended two days in the week upon Mr. Haggerstone, a dissenting minister in the neighbourhood, who had been educated under Mr. Maclaurin. Of him I learned geometry, algebra, and various branches of mathematics, theoretical and practical. And at the same time I read, but with little assistance from him, 'Gravesend's Elements of Natural Philosophy', 'Watt's Logic', 'Locke's Essay on the Human Understanding', etc, and made such a proficiency in other branches of learning, that when I was admitted at the academy (which was on Coward's foundation,) I was excused all the studies of the first year, and a great part of those of the second.

In the same interval I spent the latter part of every week with Mr. Thomas, a baptist minister, now of Bristol, but then of Gildersome, a village about four miles from Leeds, who had had no learned education. Him I instructed in Hebrew, and by that means made myself a considerable proficient in that language. At the same time I learned Chaldee and Syriac, and just began to read Arabic. Upon the whole, going to the academy later than is usual, and being thereby better furnished, I was qualified to appear there with greater advantage.

Before I went from home I was very desirous of being admitted a communicant in the congregation which I had always attended, and the old minister, as well as my aunt, was as desirous of it as myself, but the elders of the church, who had the government of it, refused me, because, when they interrogated me on the subject of the *sin of Adam*, I appeared not to be quite orthodox, not thinking that all the human race (supposing them not to have any sin of their own) were liable to the wrath of God, and the pains of hell for ever, on account of that sin only; for such was the question that was put to me. Some time before, having then no doubt of the truth of the doctrine, I well remember being much distressed that I could not feel a proper repentance for the sin of Adam; taking it for granted, that, without this, it could not be forgiven me. Mr. Haggerstone, above-mentioned, was a little more liberal than the members of the congregation in which I was brought up, being what is called a Baxterian; and his general conversation had a liberal turn, and such as tended to undermine my prejudices. But what contributed to open my eyes still more, was the conversation of a Mr. Walker, from Ashburton-under-Line, who preached as a candidate when our old minister was superannuated. He was an avowed *Baxterian,* and being rejected on that account, his opinions were much canvassed, and he being a guest at the house of my aunt, we soon became very intimate, and I thought I saw much of reason in his sentiments. Thinking further on these subjects, I was, before I went to the academy, an Arminian; but had by no means rejected the doctrine of the trinity or that of the atonement.

Though after I saw reason to change my opinion, I found myself incommoded by the rigour of the congregation with which I was connected, I shall always acknowledge, with great gratitude, that I owe much to it. The business of religion was effectually attended to in it. We were all catechised in public till we were grown up, servants as well as others, the minister always expounded the scriptures with as much regularity as he preached, and there was hardly a day in the week, in which there was not some meeting of one or other part of the congregation On one evening there was a meeting of the young men, for conversation and prayer. This I constantly attended, praying extempore with others, when called upon.

At my aunt's, there was a monthly meeting of women, who acquitted themselves in prayer as well as any of the men belonging to the congregation. Being at first a child in the family, I was permitted to attend their meetings, and growing up insensibly, heard them after I was capable of judging. My aunt, after the death of her husband, prayed every morning and evening in her family, until I was about seventeen, when that duty devolved upon me.

The Lord's day was kept with peculiar strictness. No victuals were dressed on that day in any family. No member of it was permitted to walk out for recreation, but the whole of the day was spent at the public meeting, or at home in reading, meditation, and prayer, in the family or the closet.

It was my custom at that time to recollect as much as I could of the sermons I heard, and to commit it to writing. This practice I began very early, and continued it until I was able from the heads of a discourse to supply the rest myself. For not troubling myself to commit to memory much of the amplification, and writing at home almost as much as I had heard, I insensibly acquired a habit of composing with great readiness; and from this practice I believe I have derived great advantage through life; composition seldom employing so much time as would be necessary to write in long hand any thing I have published.

By these means, not being disgusted with these strict forms of religion, as many persons of better health and spirits probably might have been, (and on which account I am far from recommending the same strictness to others) I acquired in early life a serious turn of mind. Among other things I had at this time a great aversion from *plays* and *romances*, so that I never read any works of this kind except Robinson Crusoe, until I went to the academy. I well remember seeing my brother Timothy reading a book of knight errantry, and with great indignation I snatched it out of his hands and threw it away. This brother afterwards, when he had for some time followed my father's business, (which was that of a cloth-dresser) became, if possible, more serious than I had been; and after an imperfect education, took up the profession of a minister among the Independents, in which he now continues.

While I was at the grammar school, I learned 'Mr. Annet's Short-hand', and thinking I could suggest some improvements in it, I wrote to the author, and this was the beginning of a correspondence which lasted several years. He was, as I ever perceived, an unbeliever in Christianity and a Necessarian. On this subject, several letters, written with care on both sides, passed between us, and these Mr. Annet often pressed me to give him leave to publish, but I constantly refused. I had undertaken the defence of philosophical liberty, and the correspondence was closed without my being convinced of the fallacy of my arguments, though upon studying the subject regularly, in the course of my academical education afterwards, I became a confirmed Necessarian, and I have through life derived, as I imagine, the greatest advantage from my full persuasion of the truth of that doctrine.

My aunt, and all my relations, being strict Calvinists, it was their intention to send me to the academy at Mile-End, then under the care of Dr. Cawder. But, being at that time an Arminian, I resolutely opposed it, especially upon finding that if I went thither, besides giving an *experience*, I must subscribe my assent to ten printed articles of the strictest Calvinistic faith, and repeat it every six months. My opposition, however, would probably have been to no purpose; and I must have adopted some other mode of life, if Mr. Kirkby (above-mentioned) had not interposed, and strongly recommended the academy of Dr. Doddridge, on the idea that I should have a better chance of being made a scholar. He had received a good education himself, was a good classical scholar, and had no opinion of the mode of education among the very orthodox Dissenters, and being fond of me, he was desirous of my having every advantage that could be procured for me. My good aunt, not being a bigoted Calvinist, entered into his views, and Dr. Doddridge being dead, I was sent to Daventry, and was the first pupil that entered there. My step-mother also, who was a woman of good sense, as well as of religion, had a high opinion of Dr. Doddridge, having been some time housekeeper in his family. She had always recommended his academy, but died before I went thither.

Three years, viz. from September 1752, to 1755, I spent at Daventry, with that peculiar satisfaction with which young persons of generous minds usually go through a course of liberal study, in the society of others engaged in the same pursuits, and free from the cares and anxieties which seldom fail to lay hold on them when they come out into the world.

In my time the academy was peculiarly favourable to the serious pursuit of truth, as the students were about equally divided upon every question of much importance, such as Liberty and Necessity, the sleep of the soul, and all the articles of theological orthodoxy and heresy; in consequence of which, all these topics were the subject of continual discussion. Our tutors also were of different opinions; Dr. Ashworth taking the orthodox side of every question, and Mr. Clark, the sub-tutor, that of heresy, though always with the greatest modesty.

Both of our tutors being young, at least as tutors, and some of the senior students excelling more than they could pretend to do, in several branches of study, they indulged us in the greatest freedoms, so that our lectures had often the air of friendly conversations on the subjects to which they related. We were permitted to ask whatever questions, and to make whatever remarks we pleased; and we did it with the greatest, but without any offensive, freedom. The general plan of our studies, which may be seen in Dr. Doddridge's published lectures, was exceedingly favourable to free inquiry, as we were referred to authors on both sides of every question, and were even required to give an account of them. It was also expected that we should abridge the most important of them for our future use. The public library contained all the books to which we were referred.

It was a reference to 'Dr. Hartley's Observations on Man', in the course of our Lectures, that first brought me acquainted with that performance, which immediately engaged my closest attention, and produced the greatest, and in my opinion, the most favourable effect on my general turn of thinking through life. It established me in the belief of the doctrine of necessity, which I first learned from Collins; it greatly improved that disposition to piety which I brought to the academy and freed it from the rigour with which it had been tinctured. Indeed, I do not know whether the consideration of Dr. Hartley's theory, contributes more to enlighten the mind, or improve the heart; it effects both in so super-eminent a degree.

In this situation, I saw reason to embrace what is generally called the heterodox side of almost every question.* But notwithstanding this, and though Dr. Ashworth was earnestly desirious to make me as orthodox as possible, yet, as my behaviour was unexceptionable, and as I generally took part in some little things by which he often drew upon himself the the ill-will of many of the students, I was upon the whole a favourite with him. I kept up more or less of a correspondence with Dr. Ashworth till the time of his death, though much more so with Mr. Clark. This continued till the very week of his melancholy death, by a fall from his horse at Birmingham, where he was minister.

---

* It will be seen in the course of these memoirs, that from time to time, as deeper reflection and more extensive reading incited him, he saw reason to give up almost all the peculiar theological and metaphysical opinions which he had imbibed in early youth; some of them with considerable difficulty, and all of them at the evident risk of considerable obloquy from those whom he highly respected, as well as from those on whom his interest appeared to depend. T. C.

Notwithstanding the great freedom of our speculations and debates, the extreme of heresy among us was Arianism; and all of us, I believe, left the academy with a belief, more or less qualified, of the doctrine of *atonement*.

Warm friendships never fail to be contracted at places of liberal education; and when they are well chosen, are of singular use; such was mine with Mr. Alexander of Birmingham. We were in the same class, and during the first year occupied the same room. By engagements between ourselves we rose early, and dispatched many articles of business every day. One of them, which continued all the time we were at the academy, was to read every day ten folio pages in some Greek author, and generally a Greek play in the course of the week besides. By this means we became very well acquainted with that language, and with the most valuable authors in it. This exercise we continued long after we left the academy, communicating to each other by letter an account of what we read. My life becoming more occupied than his, he continued his application to Greek longer than I did, so that before his death he was, I imagine, one of the best Greek scholars in this or any other country. My attention was always more drawn to mathematical and philosophical studies than his was.

These voluntary engagements were the more necessary, in the course of our academical studies, as there was then no provision made for teaching the learned languages. We had even no compositions or orations in latin. Our course of lectures was also defective in containing no lectures on the scriptures, or on ecclesiastical history, and by the students in general (and Mr. Alexander and myself were no exceptions) commentators in general and ecclesiastical history also, were held in contempt. On leaving the academy, he went to study under his uncle, Dr. Benson, and with him learned to value the critical study of the scriptures so much, that at length he almost confined his attention to them.

My other particular friends among my fellow students, were Mr. Henry Holland, of my own class, Messrs. Whitehead, Smithson, Rotherham, and Scholefield, in that above me; and Mr. Tayler in that below me. With all these I kept up more or less of a correspondence, and our friendship was terminated only by the death of those who are now dead, viz. the three first named of these six, and I hope it will subsist to the same period with those who now survive.

All the while I was at the academy, I never lost sight of the great object of my studies, which was the duties of a Christian minister, and there it was that I laid the general plan which I have executed since.

Particularly I there composed the first copy of my 'Institutes of Natural and Revealed Religion', Mr. Clark, to whom I communicated my scheme, carefully perusing every section of it, and talking over the subject of it with me.

But I was much discouraged even then with the *impediment in my speech,* which I inherited from my family, and which still attends me. Sometimes I absolutely stammered, and my anxiety about it was the cause of much distress to me. However, like St. Paul's *thorn in the flesh,* I hope it has not been without its use. Without some such check as this, I might have been disputatious in company, or might have been seduced by the love of popular applause as a preacher: whereas my conversation and my delivery in the pulpit having nothing in them that was generally striking, I hope I have been more attentive to qualifications of a superior kind.

It is not, I believe, usual for young persons in dissenting academies to think much of their future situation in life. Indeed, we are happily precluded from that, by the impossibility of succeeding in any application for particular places. We often, indeed, amused ourselves with the idea of our dispersion in all parts of the kingdom, after living so happily together; and used to propose plans of meeting at certain times, and smile at the different appearance we should probably make, after being ten or twenty years settled in the world. But nothing of this kind was ever seriously resolved upon by us. For my own part, I can truly say I had very little ambition, except to distinguish myself by my application to the studies proper to my profession; and I cheerfully listened to the first proposal that my tutor made to me, in consequence of an application made to him, to provide a minister for the people of Needham Market, in Suffolk, though it was very remote from my friends in Yorkshire, and a very inconsiderable place.

When I went to preach at Needham as a candidate, I found a small congregation, about an hundred people, under a Mr. Meadows, who was superannuated. They had been without a minister the preceding year, on account of the smallness of the salary; but there being some respectable and agreeable families among them, I flattered myself that I should be useful and happy in the place, and therefore accepted the unanimous invitation to be assistant to Mr. Meadows, with a view to succeed him when he died. He was a man of some fortune.

This congregation had been used to receive assistance from both the Presbyterian and Independent funds; but upon my telling them that I did not choose to have any thing to do with the Independents, and asking them whether they were able to make up the salary they promised me (which was forty pounds per annum) without any aid from the latter fund, they assured me they could. I soon, however, found that they deceived themselves; for the most that I ever received from them, was in the proportion of about thirty pounds per annum, when the expense of my board exceeded twenty pounds.

Notwithstanding this, every thing else for the first half year appeared very promising, and I was happy in the success of my schemes for promoting the interest of religion in the place. I catechised the children, though there were not many, using Dr. Watt's catechism; and I opened my lectures on the theory of religion from the 'Institutes', which I had composed at the academy, admitting all persons to attend them, without distinction of sex or age; but in this I soon found I had acted imprudently. A minister in that neighbourhood had been obliged to leave his place on account of Arianism; and though nothing had been said to me on the subject, and from the people so readily consenting to give up the Independent fund, I though they could not have much bigotry among them, I found that when I came to treat of the *Unity of God,* merely as an article of religion, several of my audience were attentive to nothing but the soundness of my faith in the doctrine of the Trinity.

Though I had made it a rule to myself to introduce nothing that could lead to controversy into the pulpit; yet making no secret of my real opinions in conversation, it was soon found that I was an Arian. From the time of this discovery, my hearers fell off apace, especially as the old minister took a decided part against me. The principal families, however, still continued with me; but notwithstanding this, my salary fell far short of thirty pounds per annum; and if it had not been for Dr. Benson and Dr. Kippis, especially the former, procuring me now and then an extraordinary five pounds, from different charities, I do not believe that I could have subsisted. I shall always remember their kindness to me at a time when I stood in so much need of it.

When I was in this situation a neighbouring minister, whose intimate friend had conformed to the church of England, talked to me on that subject. He himself, I perceived, had no great objection to it; but rejecting the proposal, as a thing that I could not think of, he never mentioned it to me any more.

To these difficulties, arising from the sentiments of my congregation, was added that of the failure of all remittances from my aunt, owing in part to the ill offices of my orthodox relations; but chiefly to her being exhausted by her liberality to others, and thinking that when I was settled in the world, I ought to be no longer burdensome to her. Together with me, she had brought up a niece, who was almost her only companion, and being deformed, could not have subsisted without the greatest part, at least, of all she had to bequeath. In consequence of these circumstances, though my aunt had always assured me that, if I chose to be a minister, she would leave me independent of the profession, I was satisfied she was not able to perform her promise, and freely consented to her leaving all she had to my cousin; I had only a silver tankard as a token of her remembrance. She had spared no expense in my education, and that was doing more for me than giving me an estate.

But what contributed greatly to my distress, was the impediment in my speech, which had increased so much, as to make preaching very painful, and took from me all chance of recommending myself to any better place. In this state, hearing of the proposal of one Mr. Angier, to cure all defects of speech, I prevailed upon my aunt to enable me to pay his price, which was twenty guineas; and this was the first occasion of my visiting London. Accordingly, I attended him about a month, taking an oath not to reveal his method, and I received some temporary benefit; but soon relapsed again, and spoke worse than ever. When I went to London, it was in company with Mr. Smithson, who was settled at Harlestown, in Norfolk. By him I was introduced to Dr. Kippis, and Dr. Benson, and by the latter to Dr. Price, but not at that time.

At Needham I felt the effect of a low despised situation, together with that arising from the want of popular talents. There were several vacancies in congregations in that neighbourhood, where my sentiments would have been no objection to me, but I was never thought of. Even my next neighbour, whose sentiments were as free as my own, and known to be so, declined making exchanges with me, which, when I left that part of the country, he acknowledged was not owing to any dislike his people had to me as heretical, but for other reasons, the more genteel part of his hearers always absenting themselves when they heard I was to preach for him. But visiting that country some years afterwards, when I had raised myself to some degree of notice in the world, and being invited to preach in that very pulpit, the same people crowded to hear me, though my elocution was not much improved, and they professed to admire one of the same discourses they had formerly despised.

Notwithstanding these unfavourable circumstances, I was far from being unhappy at Needham. I was boarded in a family from which I received much satisfaction; I firmly believed that a wise Providence was disposing every thing for the best, and I applied with great assiduity to my studies, which were classical, mathematical, and theological. These required but few books. As to experimental philosophy, I had always cultivated an acquaintance with it, but I had not the means of prosecuting it.

With respect to miscellaneous reading, I was pretty well supplied by means of a library belonging to Mr. S. Alexander, a quaker, to which I had the freest access. Here it was that I was first acquainted with any person of that persuasion; and I must acknowledge my obligation to many of them in every future stage of my life. I have met with the noblest instances of liberality of sentiment, and the truest genersoity among them.

My studies, however, were chiefly theological. Having left the academy, as I have observed, with a qualified belief of the doctrine of *atonement*, such as is found in Mr. Tomkin's book, entitled 'Jesus Christ the Mediator', I was desirous of getting some more definite ideas on the subject, and with that view set myself to peruse the whole of the 'Old and New Testament', and to collect from them all the texts that appeared to me to have any relation to the subject. This I therefore did with the greatest care, arranging them under a great variety of heads. At the same time I did not fail to note such general considerations as occurred to me while I was thus employed. The consequence of this was, what I had no apprehension of when I began the work, viz. a full persuasion that the doctrine of atonement even in its most qualified sense, had no countenance either from scripture or reason. Satisfied of this, I proceeded to digest my observations into a regular treatise, which a friend of mine, without mentioning my name, submitted to the perusal of Dr. Fleming and Dr. Lardner. In consequence of this, I was urged by them to publish the greater part of what I had written. But being then about to leave Needham, I desired them to do whatever they thought proper with respect to it, and they published about half of my piece, under the title of the 'Doctrine of Remission', &c.

This circumstance introduced me to the acquaintance of Dr. Lardner, whom I always called upon when I visited London. The last time I saw him, which was little more than a year before his death, having by letter requested him to give me some assistance with respect to the history I then prepared to write of the corruptions of Christianity, and especially that article of it, he took down a large bundle of pamphlets, and turning them over, at length shewing me my own, said, 'This contains my sentiments on the subject'. He had then forgotten that I wrote it, and on my remarking it, he shook his head, and said that his memory began to fail him; and that he had taken me for another person. He was then at the advanced age of ninety-one. This anecdote is trifling in itself, but relates to a great and good man.

I have observed that Dr. Lardner only wished to publish a part of the treatise which my friend put into his hand. The other part of it contained remarks on the reasoning of the Apostle Paul, which he could not by any means approve. They were, therefore, omitted in this publication. But the attention which I gave to the writings of this Apostle, at the time that I examined them, in order to collect passages relating to the doctrine of atonement, satisfied me that his reasoning was in many places far from being conclusive; and in a separate work I examined every passage in which his reasoning appeared to me to be defective, or his conclusions ill supported; and I thought them to be pretty numerous.

At that time I had not read any commentary on the Scriptures, except that of Mr. Henry, when I was young. However, seeing so much reason to be dissatisfied with the Apostle Paul, as a reasoner, I read 'Dr. Taylor's Paraphrase on the Epistle to the Romans', but it gave me no sort of satisfaction; and his general 'Key to the Epistles', still less. I therefore at that time wrote some remarks on it, which were a long time after published in the 'Theological Repository', vol. iv.

As I found that Dr. Lardner did not at all relish any of my observations on the imperfections of the sacred writers, I did not put this treatise into his hands; but I shewed it to some of my younger friends, and also to Dr. Kippis; and he advised me to publish it under the character of an unbeliever, in order to draw the more attention to it. This I did not chuse, having always had a great aversion to assume any character that was not my own, even so much as disputing for the sake of discovering truth. I cannot say that I was ever quite reconciled to the idea of writing to a fictitious person, as in my 'Letters to a Philosophical Unbeliever', though nothing can be more innocent, or sometimes more proper; our Saviour's parables implying a much greater departure from strict truth than those letters do. I therefore wrote the book with great freedom, indeed, but as a Christian, and an admirer of the Apostle Paul, as I always was in other respects.

When I was at Nantwich, I sent this treatise to the press; but when nine sheets were printed off, Dr. Kippis dissuaded me from proceeding, or from publishing any thing of the kind, until I should be more known, and my character better established. I therefore desisted; but when I opened the 'Theological Repository', I inserted in that work every thing that was of much consequence in the other, in order to its being submitted to the examination of learned Christians. Accordingly these communications were particularly animadverted upon by Mr. Willets, of Newcastle, under the signature of W. W. But I cannot say that his remarks gave me much satisfaction.

When I was at Needham, I likewise drew up a treatise on the doctrine of *divine influence,* having collected a number of texts for that purpose, and arranged them under proper heads, as I had done those relating to the doctrine of atonement. But I published nothing relating to it until I made use of the observations in my *sermon* on that subject, delivered at an ordination, and published many years afterwards.

While I was in this retired situation, I had, in consequence of much pains and thought, become persuaded of the falsity of the doctrine of atonement, of the inspiration of the authors of the books of Scripture as writers, and of all idea of supernatural influence, except for the purpose of miracles. But I was still an Arian, having never turned my attention to the Socinian doctrine, and contenting myself with seeing the absurdity of the Trinitarian system.

Another task that I imposed on myself, and in part executed, at Needham, was an accurate comparison of the Hebrew text of the hagiographa, and the prophets with the version of the Septuagint, noting all the variations, &c. This I had about half finished before I left that place; and I never resumed it, except to do that occasionally for particular passages, which I then began, though with many disadvantages, with a design to go through the whole. I had no polyglot Bible, and could have little help from the labours of others.

The most learned of my acquaintance in this situation, was Mr. Scott, of Ipswich, who was well versed in the Oriental languages, especially the Arabic. But though he was far from being Calvinistical, he gave me no encouragement in the very free inquiries which I then entered upon. Being excluded from all communication with the more orthodox ministers in that part of the country, all my acquaintance among the dissenting ministers, besides Mr. Scott, were Mr. Taylor of Stow-market; Mr. Dickinson of Diss; and Mr. Smithson of Harlestone: and it is rather remarkable, that we all left that country in the course of the same year; Mr. Taylor removing to Carter-lane, in London, Mr. Dickinson to Sheffield, and Mr. Smithson to Nottingham.

But I was very happy in a great degree of intimacy with Mr. Chauret, the rector of Stow-market. He was descended of French parents; and I think was not born in England. Whilst he lived, we were never long without seeing each other. But he was subject to great uneveness of spirits, sometimes the most cheerful man living, and at other times most deplorably low. In one of these fits he at length put an end to his life. I heard afterwards, that he had at one time been confined for insanity, and had even made the same attempt some time before.

Like most other young men of a liberal education, I had conceived a great aversion to the business of a schoolmaster, and had often said, that I would have recourse to any thing else for a maintenance, in preference to it. But having no other resource, I was at length compelled by necessity to make some attempt in that way; and for this purpose, I printed and distributed *proposals,* but without any effect. Not that I was thought to be unqualified for this employment, but because I was not orthodox. I had proposed to teach the classics, mathematics, &c. for half-a-guinea per quarter, and to board the pupils in the house with myself for twelve guineas per annum.

Finding this scheme not to answer, I proposed to give lectures to grown persons in such branches of science as I could conveniently procure the means of doing; and I began with reading about twelve lectures on the *use of globes,* at half-a-guinea. I had one course of ten hearers, which did something more than pay for my globes; and I should have proceeded in this way adding to my apparatus as I should have been able to afford it, if I had not left that place, which was in the following manner.

My situation being well known to my friends, Mr. Gill, a distant relation by my mother, who had taken much notice of me before I went to the academy, and had often lent me books, procured me an invitation to preach as a candidate at Sheffield, on the resignation of Mr. Wadsworth. Accordingly I did preach as a candidate, but though my opinions were no objection to me there, I was not approved. But Mr. Haynes, the other minister, perceiving that I had no chance at Sheffield, told me that he could recommend me to a congregation at Nantwich, in Cheshire, where he himself had been settled; and as it was at a great distance from Needham, he would endeavour to procure me an invitation to preach there for a year certain. This he did, and I gladly accepting of it, removed from Needham, going thence to London by sea, to save expense. This was in 1758, after having been at Needham just three years.

At Nantwich I found a good-natured friendly people, with whom I lived three years very happily; and in this situation I heard nothing of those controversies which had been the topics of almost every conversation in Suffolk; and the consequence was, that I gave little attention to them myself. Indeed it was hardly in my power to do it, on account of my engagement with a school, which I was soon able to establish, and to which I gave almost all my attention; and in this employment, contrary to my expectations, I found the greatest satisfaction, notwithstanding the confinement and labour attending it.

My school generally consisted of about thirty boys, and I had a separate room for about half a dozen young ladies. Thus I was employed from seven in the morning until four in the afternoon, without any interval, except one hour for dinner, and I never gave a holiday on any considerations, the red letter days, as they are called, excepted. Immediately after this employment in my own school rooms, I went to teach in the family of Mr. Tomkinson, an eminent attorney, and a man of large fortune, whose recommendation was of the greatest service to me; and here I continued until seven in the evening. I had therefore but little leisure for reading or for improving myself in any way, except what necessarily arose from my employment.

Being engaged in the business of a school-master, I made it my study to regulate it in the best manner, and I think I may say with truth, that in no school was more business done, or with more satisfaction, either to the master or the scholars, than in this of mine. Many of my scholars are probably living, and I am confident that they will say that this is no vain boast.

At Needham I was barely able, with the greatest economy, to keep out of debt (though this I always made a point of doing at all events) but at Nantwich my school soon enabled me to purchase a few books, and some philosophical instruments, as a small airpump, an electrical machine, &c. These I taught my scholars in the highest class to keep in order, and make use of, and by entertaining their parents and friends with experiments, in which the scholars were generally the operators, and sometimes the lecturers too, I considerably extended the reputation of my school; though I had no other object originally than gratifying my own taste. I had no lcisure, however, to make any original experiments until many years after this time.

As there were few children in the congregation, (which did not consist of more than sixty persons, and a great proportion of them travelling Scotchmen) there was no scope for exertion with respect to my duty as a minister. I therefore contented myself with giving the people what assistance I could at their own houses, where there were young persons; and I added very few sermons to those which I had composed at Needham, where I never failed to make at least one every week.

Being boarded with Mr. Eddowes, a very sociable and sensible man, and at the same time the person of the greatest property in the congregation, and who was fond of music, I was induced to learn to play a little on the English flute, as the easiest instrument; and though I was never a proficient in it, my playing contributed more or less to my amusement many years of my life. I would recommend the knowledge and practice of music to all studious persons; and it will be better for them, if, like myself, they should have no very fine ear, or exquisite taste; as by this means they will be more easily pleased, and be less apt to be offended when the performances they hear are but indifferent.

At Nantwich I had hardly any literary acquaintance besides Mr. Brereton, a clergyman in the neighbourhood, who had a taste for astronomy, philosophy, and literature in general. I often slept at his house, in a room to which he gave my name. But his conduct afterwards was unworthy of his profession.

Of dissenting ministers, I saw most of Mr. Keay, of Whitchurch, and Dr. Harwood, who lived and had a school at Congleton, preaching alternately at Leek and Wheelock, the latter place about ten miles from Nantwich. Being both of us schoolmasters, and having in some respect the same pursuits, we made exchanges for the sake of spending a Sunday evening together every six weeks in the summer time. He was a good classical scholar, and a very entertaining companion.

In my congregation there was (out of the house in which I was boarded) hardly more than one family in which I could spend a leisure hour with much satisfaction, and that was Mr. James Caldwall's, a Scotchman. Indeed, several of the travelling Scotchmen who frequented the place, but made no long stay at any time, were men of very good sense; and what I thought extraordinary, not one of them was at all Calvinistical.

My engagements in teaching allowed me but little time for composing any thing while I was at Nantwich. There, however, I recomposed my 'Observations on the Character and Reasoning of the Apostle Paul', as mentioned before. For the use of my school, I then wrote an English Grammar,* on a new plan, leaving out all such technical terms as were borrowed from other languages, and had no corresponding modifications in ours, as the future tense, &c. and to this I afterwards subjoined 'Observa-

---

* Printed in 1761.

tions for the Use of Proficients in the Language,* from the notes which I collected at Warrington; where, being tutor in the languages and Belles Letters, I gave particular attention to the English language, and intended to have composed a large treatise on the structure and present state of it. But dropping the scheme in another situation, I lately gave such parts of my collection as I had made no use of, to Mr. Herbert Croft, of Oxford, on his communicating to me his design of compiling a dictionary and grammar of our language.

The academy at Warrington was instituted when I was at Needham, and Mr. Clark knowing the attention that I had given to the learned languages when I was at Daventry, had then joined with Dr. Benson and Dr. Taylor, in recommending me as tutor in the languages. But Mr. (afterwards Dr.) Aikin, whose qualifications were superior to mine, was justly preferred to me. However, on the death of Dr. Taylor, and the advancement of Mr. Aikin to be tutor in divinity, I was invited to succeed him. This I accepted, though my school promised to be more gainful to me. But my employment at Warrington would be more liberal and less painful. It was also a means of extending my connexions. But, as I told the persons who brought me the invitation, viz. Mr. Seddon and Mr. Holland of Bolton, I should have preferred the office of teaching the mathematics and natural philosophy, for which I had at that time a great predilection.

My removal to Warrington was in September 1761, after a residence of just three years at Nantwich. In this new situation I continued six years and in the second year I married a daughter of Mr. Isaac Wilkinson, an ironmaster, near Wrexham, in Wales, with whose family I had become acquainted, in consequence of having the youngest son, William, at my school at Nantwich. This proved a very suitable and happy connexion, my wife being a woman of an excellent understanding, much improved by reading, of great fortitude and strength of mind, and of a temper in the highest degree affectionate and generous; feeling strongly for others, and little for herself. Also, greatly excelling in every thing relating to household affairs, she entirely relieved me of all concern of that kind, which allowed me to give all my time to the prosecution of my studies, and the other duties of my station. And though, in consequence of her father becoming

---

* Printed in 1772, at London. His lectures on the 'Theory of Language and Universal Grammar', were printed the same year at Warrington. David Hume was made sensible of the gallicisms and peculiarities of his style by reading this grammar. He acknowledged it to Mr. Griffith, the bookseller.

impoverished, and wholly dependent on his children, in the latter part of his life, I had little fortune with her, I unexpectedly found a great resource in her two brothers, who had become wealthy, especially the elder of them. At Warrington I had a daughter, Sarah, who was afterwards married to Mr. William Finch, of Heath Forge, near Dudley.

Though at the time of my removal to Warrington, I had no particular fondness for the studies relating to my profession then, I applied to them with great assiduity; and besides composing courses of 'Lectures on the Theory of Language', and on 'Oratory and Criticism', on which my predecessor had lectured, I introduced lectures on 'History and General Policy', on the 'Laws and Constitutions of England', and on the 'History of England'. This I did in consequence of observing that, though most of our pupils were young men designed for situations in civil and active life, every article in the plan of their education was adapted to the learned professions.

In order to recommend such studies as I introduced, I composed an 'Essay on a Course of Liberal Education for Civil and Active Life', with 'Syllabuses' of my three new courses of lectures; and Dr. Brown having just then published a plan of education, in which he recommended it to be undertaken by the state, I added some 'Remarks on his Treatise', shewing how inimical it was to liberty, and the natural rights of parents. This leading me to consider the subject of civil and political liberty, I published my thoughts on it, in an 'Essay on Government', which in a second edition I much enlarged, including in it what I wrote in answer to Dr. Balguy, on church authority, as well as my animadversions on Dr. Brown.

My 'Lectures on the Theory of Language and Universal Grammar', were printed for the use of the students, but they were not published. Those on 'Oratory and Criticism', I published when I was with Lord Shelburne; and those on 'History and General Polocy', are now printed, and about to be published.*

Finding no public exercises at Warrington, I introduced them there, so that afterwards every Saturday the tutors, all the students, and often strangers, were assembled to hear English and Latin compositions, and sometimes, to hear the delivery of speeches, and the exhibition of scenes in plays. It was my province to teach elocution and also logic, and Hebrew.

---

* This work has been reprinted in Philadelphia, with additions, particularly of a chapter on the government of the United States.

The first of these I retained; but after a year or two I exchanged the two last articles with Dr. Aikin, for the civil law, and one year I gave a course of lectures in anatomy.

With a view to lead the students to a facility in writing English, I encouraged them to write in verse. This I did not with any design to make them poets, but to give them a greater facility in writing prose, and this method I would recommend to all tutors. I was myself far from having any pretension to the character of a poet; but in the early part of my life, I was a great versifier, and this, I believe, as well as my custom of writing after preachers, mentioned before, contributed to the ease with which I always wrote prose. Mrs. Barbauld has told me that it was the perusal of some verses of mine, that first induced her to write any thing in verse, so that this country is in some measure indebted to me for one of the best poets it can boast of. Several of her first poems were written when she was in my house, on occasions that occurred while she was there.

It was while I was at Warrington, that I published my 'Chart of Biography', though I had begun to construct it at Nantwich. Lord Willoughby of Parham, who lived in Lancashire, being pleased with the idea of it, I, with his consent, inscribed it to him; but he died before the publication of it: the 'Chart of History', corresponding to it, I drew up some time after at Leeds.

I was in this situation, when, going to London,* and being introduced to Dr. Price, Mr. Canton, Dr. Watson, (the physician) and Dr. Franklin, I was led to attend to the subject of experimental philosophy, more than I had done before; and having composed all the lectures I had occasion to deliver, and finding myself at liberty for any undertaking, I mentioned to Dr. Franklin an idea that had occurred to me of writing the history of discoveries in electricity, which had been his favourite study. This I told him might be an useful work, and that I would willingly undertake it, provided I could be furnished with the books necessary for the purpose. This he readily undertook, and my other friends assisting him in it, I set about the work, without having the least idea of doing any thing more than writing a distinct and methodical account of all that had been done by others. Having, however, a pretty good machine, I was led, in the

---

* He always spent one month in every year in London, which was of great use to him. He saw and heard a great deal. He generally made additions to his library, and his chemical apparatus. A new turn was frequently given to his ideas. New and useful acquaintances were formed, and old ones confirmed.

course of my writing the history, to endeavour to ascertain several facts which were disputed; and this led me by degrees into a large field of original experiments, in which I spared no expense that I could possibly furnish.

These experiments employed a great proportion of my leisure time; and yet before the complete expiration of the year, in which I gave the plan of my work to Dr. Franklin, I sent him a copy of it in print. In the same year, five hours of every day were employed in lectures, public or private, and one two months vacation I spent chiefly at Bristol, on a visit to my father-in-law.

This I do not mention as a subject of boasting. For many persons have done more in the same time; but as an answer to those who have objected to some of my later writings, as hasty performances. For none of my publications were better received than this 'History of Electricity', which was the most hasty of them all. However, whether my publications have taken up more or less time, I am confident that more would not have contributed to their perfection, in any essential particular; and about any thing farther I have never been very solicitous. My object was not to acquire the character of a fine writer, but of an useful one. I can also truly say, that gain was never the chief object of any of my publications. Several of them were written with the prospect of certain loss.

During the course of my electrical experiments in this year, I kept up a constant correspondence with Dr. Franklin, and the rest of my philosophical friends in London; and my letters circulated among them all, as also every part of my history as it was transcribed. This correspondence would have made a considerable volume, and it took up much time; but it was of great use with respect to the accuracy of my experiments, and the perfection of my work.

After the publication of my 'Chart of Biography', Dr. Percival of Manchester, then a student at Edinburgh, procured me the title of Doctor of Laws, from that university,; and not long after my new experiments in electricity were the means of introducing me into the Royal Society, with the recommendation of Dr. Franklin, Dr. Watson, Mr. Canton, and Dr. Price.

In the whole time of my being at Warrington, I was singularly happy in the society of my fellow tutors,* and of Mr. Seddon, the minister of the

---

* At Warrington he had for colleagues and successors, Dr. John Taylor, author of the 'Hebrew Concordance', and of several other works, on 'Original Sin',

place. We drank tea together every Saturday, and our convention was
equally instructive and pleasing. I often thought it not a little extraordinary,
that four persons, who had no previous knowledge of each other, should
have been brought to unite in conducting such a scheme as this, and all
be zealous Necessarians, as we were. We were likewise all Arians, and the
only subject of much consequence on which we differed, was respecting the
doctrine of atonement, concerning which Dr. Aikin held some obscure
notions. Accordingly, this was frequently the topic of our friendly conversations. The only Socinian in the neighbourhood was Mr. Seddon, of
Manchester; and we all wondered at him. But then we never entered into
any particular examination of the subject.

Receiving some of the pupils into my own house, I was by this means led
to form some valuable friendships, but especially with Mr. Samuel
Vaughan, a friendship which has continued hitherto, has in a manner
connected our families, and will, I doubt not, continue through life. The
two eldest of his sons were boarded with me.

The tutors having sufficient society among themselves, we had not much
acquaintance out of the academy. Sometimes, however, I made an excursion
to the towns in the neighbourhood. At Liverpool I was always received by
Mr. Bentley, afterwards partner with Mr. Wedgwood, a man of excellent
taste, improved understanding, and a good disposition, but an unbeliever
in Christianity, which was therefore often the subject of our conversations.
He was then a widower, and we generally, and contrary to my usual
custom, sat up late. At Manchester I was always the guest of Mr. Potter,
whose son Thomas was boarded with me. He was one of the worthiest
men that ever lived. At Chowbent I was much acquainted with Mr. Mort,
a man equally distinguished, by his cheerfulness and liberality of
sentiment.

Of the ministers in the neighbourhood, I recollect with much satisfaction
the interviews I had with Mr. Godwin, of Gateacre, Mr. Holland, of
Bolton, and Dr. Enfield, of Liverpool, afterwards tutor at Warrington.

Though all the tutors in my time lived in the most perfect harmony,
though we all exerted ourselves to the utmost, and there was no complaint
of want of discipline, the academy did not flourish. There had been an
unhappy difference between Dr. Taylor and the trustees, in consequence of

---

'Atonement', &c. Dr. Aikin the elder, Dr. Reinhold Forster, the naturalist
and traveller, Dr. Enfield, and Mr. Walker.

which all his friends, who were numerous, were our enemies; and too many of the subscribers, being probably weary of the subscription, were willing to lay hold of any pretence for dropping it, and of justifying their conduct afterwards.

It is possible that in time we might have overcome the prejudices we laboured under; but there being no prospect of things being any better, and my wife having very bad health, on her account chiefly I wished for a removal, though nothing could be more agreeable to me at the time than the whole of my employment, and all the laborious part of it was over. The terms also on which we took boarders, being fifteen pounds per annum, and my salary being only one hundred pounds per annum,, with a house, it was not possible, even living with the greatest frugality, to make any provision for a family. I was there six years, most laboriously employed, for nothing more than a bare subsistence. I therefore listened to an invitation to take the charge of the congregation of Mill-hill chapel, at Leeds, where I was pretty well known, and thither I removed in September, 1767.

Though while I was at Warrington, it was no part of my duty to preach, I had from choice continued the practice; and wishing to keep up the character of a dissenting minister, I chose to be ordained while I was there; and though I was far from having conquered my tendency to stammer, and probably never shall be able to do it effectually, I had, by taking much pains, improved my pronunciation some time before I left Nantwich; where, for the first two years, this impediment had increased so much, that I once informed the people that I must give up the business of preaching, and confine myself to my school. However, by making a practice of reading very loud and very slow every day, I at length succeeded in getting some measure the better of this defect; but I am still obliged occasionally to have recourse to the same expedient.

At Leeds I continued six years very happy with a liberal, friendly, and harmonious congregation, to whom my services, (of which I was not sparing) were very acceptable. Here I had no unreasonable prejudices to contend with, so that I had full scope for every kind of exertion; and I can truly say that I always considered the office of a Christian minister as the most honourable of any upon earth, and in the studies proper to it I always took the greatest pleasure.

In this situation I naturally resumed my application to speculative theology, which had occupied me at Needham, and which had been interrupted by the business of teaching at Nantwich and Warrington. By reading with care, 'Dr. Lardner's Letter on the Logos', I became what is called a Socinian soon after my settlement at Leeds; and after giving the closest attention to the subject, I have seen more and more reason to be satisfied with that opinion to this day, and likewise to be more impressed with the idea of its importance.

On reading Mr. Mann's 'Dissertation on the Times of the Birth and Death of Christ', I was convinced that he was right in his opinion of our Saviour's ministry, having continued little more than one year, and on this plan I drew out a 'Harmony of the Gospels', the outline of which I first published in the 'Theological Repository', and afterwards separately and at large, both in Greek and English, with notes, and an occasional paraphrase. In the same work I published my 'Essay on the Doctrine of Atonement', improved from the tract published by Dr. Lardner, and also my animadversions on the reasoning of the Apostle Paul.

The plan of this 'Repository' occurred to me on seeing some notes that Mr. Turner, of Wakefield, had drawn up on several passages of Scripture, which I was concerned to think should be lost. He very much approved of my proposal of an occasional publication, for the purpose of preserving such original observations as could otherwise probably never see the light. Of this work I published three volumes while I was at Leeds, and he never failed to give me an article for every number of which they were composed.

Giving particular attention to the duties of my office, I wrote several tracts for the use of my congregation, as two 'Catechisms', an 'Address to Masters of Families on the Subject of Family Prayer', a 'Discourse on the Lord's Supper', and on 'Church Discipline', and 'Institutes of Natural and Revealed Religion'. Here I formed three classes of catechumens, and took great pleasure in instructing them in the principles of religion. In this respect I hope my example has been of use in other congregations.

The first of my controversial treatises was written here in reply to some angry remarks on my 'Discourse on the Lord's Supper', by Mr. Venn, a clergyman in the neighbourhood. I also wrote 'Remarks on Dr. Balguy's Sermon on Church Authority', and on some paragraphs in Judge 'Blackstone's Commentaries', relating to the Dissenters. To the two former no reply was made; but to the last the judge replied in a small pamphlet; on which I addressed a letter to him in the 'St. James's Chronicle'. This controversy led me to print another pamphlet, entitled 'The Principles and Conduct of the Dissenters, with respect to the Civil and Ecclesiastical Constitution of the Country'. With the encouragement of Dr. Price and Dr. Kippis, I also wrote an 'Address to Protestant Dissenters as such'; but without my name. Several of these pamphlets having been animadverted upon by an anonymous acquaintance, who thought I laid too much stress on the principles of the Dissenters, I wrote a defence of my conduct in letters addressed to him.

The Methodists being very numerous in Leeds, and many of the lower sort of my own hearers listening to them, I wrote 'An Appeal to the Serious Professors of Christianity', 'An Illustration of Particular Texts', and republished the 'Trial of Elwall', all in the cheapest manner possible. Those small tracts had a great effect in establishing my hearers in liberal principles of religion, and in a short time had a far more extensive influence than I could have imagined. By this time more than thirty thousand copies of the 'Appeal', have been dispersed.

Besides these theoretical and controversial pieces, I wrote while I was at Leeds, my 'Essay on Government', mentioned before; my 'English Grammar', enlarged; a 'Familiar Introduction to the Study of Electricity'; a 'Treatise on Perspective'; and my 'Chart of History'; and also some anonymous pieces in favour of civil liberty during the persecution of Mr. Wilkes, the principal of which was 'An Address to Dissenters on the Subject of the Difference with America', which I wrote at the request of Dr. Franklin, and Dr. Fothergil.

But nothing of a nature foreign to the duties of my profession engaged my attention while I was at Leeds so much as the prosecution of my experiments relating to electricity, and especially the doctrine of air. The last I was led into in consequence of inhabiting a house adjoining to a public brewery, where I at first amused myself with making experiments on the fixed air which I found ready made in the process of fermentation. When I removed from that house, I was under the necessity of making the fixed air for myself; and one experiment leading to another, as I have distinctly and faithfully noted in my various publications on the subject I by degrees contrived a convenient apparatus for the purpose, but of the cheapest kind.

When I began these experiments, I knew very little of chemistry, and had in a manner no idea on the subject before I attended a course of chemical lectures, delivered in the academy at Warrington, by Dr. Turner, of Liverpool. But I have often thought that upon the whole, this circumstance was no disadvantage to me; as in this situation I was led to devise an apparatus, and processes of my own, adapted to my peculiar views. Whereas, if I had been previously accustomed to the usual chemical processes, I should not have so easily thought of any other; and without

new modes of operation I should hardly have discovered any thing new.*
My first publication on the subject of air was in 1772. It was a small
pamphlet, on the method of impregnating water with fixed air; which
being immediately translated into French, excited a great degree of
attention to the subject, and this was much increased by the publication
of my first paper of experiments, in a large article of the 'Philosophical
Transactions', the year following, for which I received the gold medal of
the Society. My method of impregnating water with fixed air, was considered at a meeting of the College of Physicians, before whom I made the
experiments, and by them it was recommended to the Lords of the
Admiralty, (by whom they had been summoned for the purpose) as likely
to be of use in the sea scurvy.

The only person in Leeds who gave much attention to my experiments
was Mr. Hey, a surgeon. He was a zealous Methodist, and wrote answers to
some of my theological tracts; but we always conversed with the greatest
freedom on philosophical subjects, without mentioning any thing relating
to theology. When I left Leeds, he begged of me the earthen trough in
which I had made all my experiments on air while I was there. It was such
an one as is there commonly used for washing linen.

Having succeeded so well in the 'History of Electricity', I was induced to
undertake the history of all the branches of experimental philosophy; and
at Leeds I gave out proposals for that purpose, and published the 'History
of Discoveries relating to Vision, Light, and Colours'. This work, also, I
believe I executed to general satisfaction, and being an undertaking of
great expense, I was under the necessity of publishing it by subscription.
The sale, however, was not such as to encourage me to proceed with a work
of so much labour and expense; so that after purchasing a great number of
books, to enable me to finish my undertaking, I was obliged to abandon
it, and to apply wholly to original experiments.

In writing the History of Discoveries relating to Vision, I was much
assisted by Mr. Michell, the discoverer of the method of making artificial
magnets. Living at Thornhill, not very far from Leeds, I frequently visited

---

* This necessary attention to economy, also aided the simplicity of his apparatus,
and was the means in some degree of improving it in this important respect.
This plainess of his apparatus rendered his experiments easy to be repeated,
and gave them accuracy. In this respect, he was like his great contemporary,
Scheele, whose discoveries were made by means easy to be procured, and at
small expense. The French chemists have adopted a practice quite the
reverse.

him, and was very happy in his society, as I also was in that of Mr. Smeaton, who lived still nearer to me. He made me a present of his excellent air pump, which I constantly use to this day. Having strongly recommended his construction of this instrument, it is now generally used; whereas before that, hardly any had been made during the twenty years which had elapsed after the account that he had given of it in the 'Philosophical Transactions'.

I was also instrumental in reviving the use of large electrical machines, and batteries, in electricity, the generality of electrical machines being little more than play things at the time that I began my experiments. The first very large electrical machine was made by Mr. Nairne, in consequence of a request made to me by the Grand Duke of Tuscany, to get him the best machine that we could make in England. This, and another that he made for Mr. Vaughan, were constituted on a plan of my own. But afterwards Mr. Nairne made large machines on a more simple and improved construction; and in consideration of the service which I had rendered him, he made me a present of a pretty large machine of the same kind.

The review of my 'History of Electricity', by Mr. Bewley, who was acquainted with Mr. Michell, was the means of opening a correspondence between us, which was the source of much satisfaction to me as long as he lived. I instantly communicated to him an account of every new experiment that I made, and, in return, was favoured with his remarks upon them. All that he published of his own were articles in the 'Appendixes' to my volumes on air, all of which are ingenious and valuable. Always publishing in this manner, he used to call himself my *satellite*. There was a vein of pleasant wit and humour in all his correspondence, which added greatly to the value of it. His letters to me would have made several volumes, and mine to him still more. When he found himself dangerously ill, he made a point of paying me a visit before he died; and he made a journey from Norfolk to Birmingham, accompanied by Mrs. Bewley, for that purpose; and after spending about a week with me, he went to his friend, Dr. Burney, and at this house he died.

While I was at Leeds, a proposal was made to me, to accompany Captain Cook in his second voyage to the South Seas. As the terms were very advantageous, I consented to it, and the heads of my congregation had agreed to keep an assistant to supply my place during my absence. But Mr. Banks informed me that I was objected to by some clergymen in the Board of Longitude, who had the direction of his business, on account of my religious principles; and presently after I heard that Dr. Forster, a person far better qualified for the purpose, had got the appointment. As I had barely acquiesced in the proposal, this was no disappointment to me, and I was much better employed at home, even with respect to my philosophical pursuits. My knowledge of natural history was not sufficient for the undertaking; but at that time I should, by application, have been able to supply my deficiency, though now I am sensible I could not do it. At Leeds I was particularly happy in my intercourse with Mr. Turner, of Wakefield, and occasionally, with Mr. Cappe, of York; and Mr. Graham, of Halifax. And here it was that in consequence of a visit which in company with Mr. Turner I made to the Archdeacon Blackburne, at Richmond, (with whom I had kept up a correspondence from the time that his son was under my care at Warrington) I first met with Mr. Lindsey, then of Catterick, and a correspondence and intimacy commenced, which has been the source of more real satisfaction to me than any other circumstance in my whole life. He soon discovered to me that he was uneasy in his situation, and had thoughts of quitting it. At first I was not forward to encourage him in it, but rather advised him to make what alteration he thought proper in the offices of the church, and leave it to his superiours to dismiss him if they chose. But his better judgement, and greater fortitude, led him to give up all connexion with the established church of his own accord.

This took place about the time of my leaving Leeds, and it was not until long after this, that I was apprised of all the difficulties he had to struggle with before he could accomplish his purpose. But the opposition made to it by his nearest friends, and those who might have been expected to approve of the step that he took, and to have endeavoured to make it easy to him, was one of the greatest. Notwithstanding this, he left Catterick, where he had lived in affluence, idolised by his parish, and went to London without any certain prospect, where he lived in two rooms on a ground floor, until by the assistance of his friends, he was able to pay for the use of the upper apartments, which the state of his health rendered necessary. In this humble situation have I passed some of the most pleasing hours of my life; when, in consequence of living with Lord Shelburne, I spent my winters in London.

On this occasion it was that my intimacy with Mr. Lindsey was much improved, and an entire concurrence in every thing that we thought to be for the interest of Christianity, gave fresh warmth to our friendship. To his society I owe much of my zeal for the doctrine of the divine unity, for which he made so great sacrifices, and in the defence of which he so

D

much distinguished himself, so as to occasion a new era in the history of religion in this country.

As we became more intimate, confiding in his better taste and judgment, and also in that of Mrs. Lindsey, a woman of the same spirit and views, and in all respects a help-meet for him, I never chose to publish any thing of moment relating to theology, without consulting him; and hardly ever ventured to insert any thing that they disapproved, being sensible that my disposition led to precipitancy, to which their coolness was a seasonable check.

At Leeds began my intercourse with Mr. Lee, of Lincoln's Inn. He was a native of the place, and exactly one week older than myself. At that time he was particularly connected with the congregation, and before he was married spent his vacations with us. His friendship was a source of much greater satisfaction and advantage to me after I came to reside in London, and especially at the time of my leaving Lord Shelburne, when my prospects wore rather a cloudy aspect.

When I visited London, during my residence at Leeds, commenced my particular friendship for Dr. Price, to whom I had been introduced several years before by Dr. Benson; our first interview having been at Mr. Brownsword's, at Newington, where they were members of a small literary society, in which they read various compositions. At that time Dr. Benson read a paper which afterwards made a section in his 'Life of Christ'. For the most amiable simplicity of character, equalled only by that of Mr. Lindsey, a truly Christian spirit, disinterested patriotism, and true candour, no man in my opinion ever exceeded Dr. Price. His candour will appear the more extraordinary, considering his warm attachments to the theological sentiments which he embraced in very early life. I shall ever reflect upon our friendship as a circumstance highly honourable, as it was a source of peculiar satisfaction to me.

I had two sons born to me at Leeds, Joseph and William, and though I was very happy there, I was tempted to leave it after continuing there six years, to go into the family of the Earl of Shelburne, now the Marquis of Lansdowne; he stipulating to give me two hundred and fifty pounds per annum, a house to live in, and a certainty for life in case of his death, or of my separation from him; whereas at Leeds my salary was only one hundred guineas per annum, and a house, which was not quite sufficient for the subsistence of my family, without a possibility of making a provision for them after my death.

I had been recommended to Lord Shelburne by Dr. Price, as a person qualified to be a literary companion to him. In this situation, my family being at Calne, in Wiltshire, near to his lordship's seat at Bowood, I continued seven years, spending the summer with my family, and a great part of the winter in his Lordship's house in London. My office was nominally that of *Librarian*, but I had little employment as such, besides arranging his books, taking a catalogue of them, and of his manuscripts, which were numerous, and making an index to his collection of private papers. In fact I was with him as a friend, and the second year made with him the tour of Flanders, Holland, and Germany, as far as Strasburgh; and after spending a month at Paris, returned to England. This was in the year 1774. . . .

A Journal of a Tour through Flanders, Holland, Part of Germany, and France

(PARTLY IN THE FORM OF THREE LETTERS TO THE SONS OF LORD SHELBURNE)

Lisle, August 26, 1774.

Dear Mr. Petty,

As I am sure your curiosity is not less than your brother's, I shall endeavour to gratify it by resuming our journal where your papa left off.

I was very much struck with the appearance of Calais, as it was the first fortified town I had ever seen; being surrounded with a deep ditch and strong walls, built in such a manner as to make it very difficult to be taken by an enemy. St. Omers, Aire, Bethune, and Lisle, which we have seen since, are all fortified in the same manner; and they have all spacious market places, where the inhabitants may be assembled, and where the soldiers can parade. All these towns are much better built than the generality of towns in England. In Lisle, especially, the houses are curiously ornamented towards the street with figures of heads, festoons, and other decorations. The rooms in the inns which we have seen are exceedingly large and lofty; and the furniture, though it has, in some respect, the air of great magnificence, is in general ill made, and not elegant; most things being finished in a manner that we should be ashamed of in England. Their fire-places are much unlike ours, but pretty enough, and they are all made for the burning of wood, as the country produces no coal.

Having dined at Calais, we reached St. Omers, but not till after it was dark; by which means we were deprived of the sight of a good part of the country, which has improved upon us ever since we left Calais. In the neighbourhood of that place we found the ground miserably neglected, and yielding hardly any thing at all. We were particularly surprised to find a great deal of hay in the fields, some just mowed, and a field of oats quite green. But every thing wore a much better aspect as we advanced further into the country; and yesterday, in which we travelled from St. Omers to Lisle, we saw every where the finest cultivation possible, and the harvest nearly got in. It seemed to be much superior to the generality of English husbandry; but we have yet seen no inclosures, and hardly any grass or meads, cows or sheep; these being fed in places where the soil is not so rich. At Bethune we were amused as we went through the market with the sight of a number of the slenderest and leanest pigs we had ever seen. They might almost have been taken for greyhounds. The horses we have seen are, in general, small, lean, and not at all handsome; but, notwithstanding, very active, and do their business very well. You would have smiled if you could have been with us this morning, and seen, as I did, dogs drawing little carts with very considerable loads, and men drawing sedan chairs mounted on wheels. By this means, however, people are very well carried, and one man does the work of two with us.

All the way we have come, we were surprised at the prodigious quantity of tall, fine beans, which are all standing, and especially with the plantations of tobacco and poppies, which are not cultivated in England. The tobacco was very green, and looked exceedingly beautiful; the poppies were all reaped and formed into sheaves or rocks. We could not imagine of what use so much poppy seed could be, but upon inquiry we were informed that they get a great deal of oil from them, and that the many windmills we saw in the neighbourhood were all employed to press that oil, which is used for lamps.

Though you are not a man of gallantry, yet, as you are an observer of human nature, I must tell you what has struck me most relating to the women we have seen. Many of them, even those who are well dressed, walk the street in slippers, without any thing to cover the heel; so that, except the toe, the whole foot is seen as they walk, which to me, who never saw the like before, looked slatternly and indelicate. Almost all the women are dressed in what we call a French night-cap, which almost covers their cheeks; and we saw a great number of country women going to and from the market of Bethune, many of them in carts, with their heads dressed particularly neat; but not one of them had any hat to screen them from the sun or rain; nor have we seen one woman with a hat on since we left

England. By this means they soon get sunburned and look ugly, while the men wear large hats and save their faces. Instead of cloaks, the women of all ranks have a square piece of cloth or stuff which they throw over their shoulders or their heads at pleasure; and sometimes it is so large as to reach almost to their feet. Betwixt Lisle and Ghent, which we reached on Saturday, the country women were provided with straw bonnets, which, though not very elegant, must be very convenient. All the better sort of people, men as well as women, when they walk out in the sun or the rain, hold an umbrella in their hands, and sometimes one of them will serve for two persons. A number of these umbrellas have a very pretty appearance in a street, especially as they are of different colours, and the fashion of them is elegant; but they would by no means do in the streets of London, or any crowded place; for they necessarily take up a good deal of room.

At Lisle, you, as having a military turn, would have received great pleasure from what was not only irksome, but a cause of a good deal of pain to me. This was the review of a regiment of French soldiers in compliment to your papa. They did not fire, but they performed a variety of new and very useful evolutions lately introduced by the King of Prussia. The pain that I felt on this occasion did not arise from any consideration of the mischief that this new discipline might enable the French to do us in any future war, but from a cold that I got at the time, which affected my teeth very much.

Being suddenly called to close my letter by an opportunity that just offers of sending it to England, I can only conclude with assuring you that this journal shall be continued, and that I shall think myself very happy if it contributes to your amusement.

With the greatest affection, I am, dear Mr. Petty, yours sincerely.

Brussels, 30th August, 1774.

I beg my respectful compliments to Lord Fitzmaurice and Mr. Jervis.

Amsterdam, Sep. 6, 1774.

My dear Lord Fitzmaurice,

Your brother will, I hope, before this time, have communicated to you the account I sent him of our travels as far as Lisle, and it is with great pleasure that I now sit down to send you an account of our progress from thence to Amsterdam, where we now are, and where we propose to stay for a few days.

We left Lisle on Saturday, the 27th of August, and passing through Menin and Courtray, both fortified towns, arrived at Ghent before dinner, and from thence we set out the next day and arrived at Brussels before night. There we waited upon the Duke d'Aremberg and dined with him in town the next day, and the day following in the country, at Engyen, about fifteen miles from Brussels.

On Thursday, the first of September, we left Brussels, and passing through Mechlin, got to Antwerp before dinner; and setting out from thence early the next morning, we arrived, after a very fatiguing journey, at Rotterdam, but in the dark.

The whole of Austrian Flanders is highly cultivated and populous. The farm-houses seemed to be substantially good, and the poorest people we met, tolerably well clothed. Indeed, we have not yet seen people so exceedingly shabby and wretched as the poor of Calne. It is something remarkable, however, that in this country the boys on the wayside have the same ridiculous custom of tumbling and standing on their heads that you will see at Studley, and which I have also seen in one part of Yorkshire. But here we once saw a girl standing on her head for this purpose. You may be assured that we did not encourage so much idleness and indecency by giving them any thing, though the custom could not have been established, if others had not been diverted with it and countenanced it.

This country has formerly produced very excellent painters, especially the celebrated Rubens; and though (which is very remarkable) they can boast of no painters at present, the rich and curious give immense sums for pictures to furnish their cabinets, and some make a gainful traffic of buying to sell again. A curious character of this kind we met with at Ghent, who took not little pains, and used a good deal of address, to take in your papa. We got a sight of his pictures over night, and as he was very importunate, partly promised to see him again the next morning. However, as we were walking in the church, the next morning, which was Sunday, we happened to pass by a confessional chair where he was confessing an old woman; and the moment he cast his eyes upon us, he gave us an intimation that he would be with us immediately; and so despatching his penitent with a most indecent hurry, he presently joined us. It was then impossible to avoid going to his house, from whence we returned, truly pleased with many of his pictures; more with so curious a character; and most of all that we saw through his artifice, and did not contribute to gratify his covetousness at our expense.

Another adventure of this kind we had at Antwerp. One of these trafficking connoisseurs shewed us a picture as an original of Rubens, and asked a prodigious price for it. Our guide, who, no doubt, was in league with him, avouched it; but going immediately from thence to the house of a rich and whimsical canon, we saw the real original of the very same picture, the same guide conducting us. This canon also was a much greater curiosity himself than any thing he had to shew. He had no real knowledge of any thing he had got, but had a valet who shewed them; and we were told, that sometimes when such questions were asked, as he could not answer himself, he would send for his maid. Indeed, his valet made so very free, both his master and us, as made any thing of this kind very credible. This canon was very eager to hear every thing about him admired, but affected to make a great secret of every thing, and, in the bluntest and rudest manner, said *no* to almost every question your papa asked him about the management of his flowers, &c.; and though we particularly admired some fine peaches that he had got, he would not understand the hint so far as to desire our acceptance of one; and had we directly asked him for one, as your papa, for curiosity, had once thought of doing, I doubt not he would have again said *no*; which was a monosyllable that seemed very familiar to him. Two such characters as those of these canons can hardly be found except in such seclusion from the world, and such an independence on others, as is peculiar to the Romish clergy.

From Alost to Brussels we saw many hops, and, I think, finer than any we had seen as we travelled through Kent. The beer of this country is by no means so good as in England.

The country we are now in is in many respects different from that of Flanders, but my paper admonishes me to conclude, and write a continuation at another opportunity.

I am, with compliments to Mr. Petty and Mr. Jervis, my dear Lord, your affectionate, humble servant.

P.S. Your papa is very well, and sends his love to your brother.

Paris, Oct. 6, 1774.

Dear Mr. Petty,

I was very sorry to hear of your misfortune, but hope that by this time you feel no disagreeable remains of it. I hope the inclosed journal will contribute to amuse you, and to convince you that I am, with great respect, my dear friend, your affectionate, humble servant.

We took our leave of Flanders on Friday, the 2nd of September, and crossing an arm of the sea at Mardyke, arrived at Rotterdam after it was dark; the lights in the town having a very agreeable effect across the water, over which we passed to come to it.

Holland seems to be surrounded either by the *sea,* or an absolute *desert.*
Such, however, is the boundary that we passed on the side of Flanders,
and also on the side of Germany, and, both these sides, are as unpassable
as *sand* can make them. We had on this account most tiresome travelling,
both into this country and out of it.

We spent the morning of Saturday the 3rd, in walking about Rotterdam,
and seeing what was most worth seeing in it; and after dinner we went in
the Trackschyt by Delft, (where we stopped to see a magnificent tomb of
the Prince of Orange), to Leyden. The next morning we saw the physic
garden in this place; then went by Woder to Haarlem, where we heard the
famous organ, during the time of divine service, and went in two small
carriages by land to Alcmaer, where we arrived just at dark. In this journey
we skirted that part of Holland which is occupied by sand-hills, along the
coast of the German Ocean. This tract of hilly ground seems to be of no
use but to keep off the sea. In one place we saw there had been an attempt
to sow a little barley in it, but the produce had not been worth reaping.

On Monday we set out in an awkward kind of carriage that held four
persons, and dining at Purmeren, and stopping to see the village of Brook
we got to Amsterdam before night. We have intended to have seen the
famous dykes that keep off the sea, and also Saardam, where most of the
Dutch ships are built; but we were disappointed by our guides, who after
having pocketed the money for that tour, took us another and a shorter
way; and had our lives depended upon it, instead of the gratifying of our
curiosity, I almost think those Dutchmen would have done just the same
thing, and with the same coolness and self-applause. But, for the honour
of human nature, I am willing to think we should not have been served so
in any other country.

Though it is probable that the commerce and power of this country is
upon the decline, the harbour of Amsterdam is really a most astonishing
sight. Such a number of ships is, I believe, no where else to be found in
one place. The Town House also quite astonished me, both for the expence
and magnificence of that part of it which is always open to every body,
(being all cased with marble, disposed in excellent taste and exquisite
workmanship), and for the noble suite and furniture of the rooms adapted
to all kinds of public business.

We were also much pleased with the rope-house and stow-house of the
East India Company; but, excepting these, and a few good pictures, which
we saw at Mr. Hope's, with whom we dined on Wednesday, we saw nothing
worth particular notice in this place, which, upon the whole, is a very

disagreeable one. We therefore left it on Thursday, which was sooner than we had intended, and came by water to Utretcht in the dark. There we joined the cook, who had been sent thither from Rotterdam with the coach. In this passage we were much amused with the view of the Dutch country houses, with which this canal, (as also that which led from Delft to Leyden), was lined. Some of them were old-fashioned, dark, and gloomy retreats, suitable enough, in my opinion, for those who had amassed a fortune in such a manner as is generally ascribed to this industrious, but selfish people. But in others there was real elegance and good taste, with a general uniformity, (especially in long straight vistas of trees, some covered and some open, and all most exactly cut and trimmed), amidst a very great and whimsical variety. Some of them must have been exceedingly expensive, and equal to those of very rich country gentlemen in England.

On Friday we left Utrecht, intending to have reached Nimeguen before night; but we found the roads so intolerably heavy, that we were obliged to lodge at a small place called Grip; so we dined at Nimeguen the next day, and got to Cleef, in the King of Prussia's dominions, that night; taking leave, to our great satisfaction, of the country and people of Holland.

Although, however, it must be allowed that Holland is a great curiosity, and well worth the transient visit of a statesman, or a philosopher, though it is certainly the last in which a man of a liberal turn of mind would choose to live.

There people here are so much occupied with commerce, that agriculture is no object of attention with them. We hardly saw a single field of corn in Holland, all the ground being employed in pasture. But though the cattle do not look ill, the horses are not capable of much service, and the flesh of their oxen and sheep is of a loose texture, and without flavour. This is owing, I suppose, to the marshiness of their meadows, and the very bad water they are obliged to drink. Indeed, the whole country of Holland does not afford any water that a man can well drink. This circumstance, at least, furnishes them with an excuse for drinking wine and spirituous liquors in great quantities, and also for smoking tobacco, with which they almost poison every body that comes near them. Indeed, I can hardly express how very low, beastly, and sordid, the manners of the common people in this country are. It is a thing very different from the roughness and brutality of some of the low-bred people of England. In Germany or France, as far as I can observe, neither of those characters, which are the disgrace of human nature, exists.

Upon the whole, we are much disgusted with the people of Holland, and their manners; and were glad to get into the more open air, and more natural and agreeable manners of Germany.

[*The Journal continued*]

On leaving Holland we felt ourselves elevated, as if we were emerging from a low and heavy atmosphere into a superior region, where we fancied we breathed more freely than before; and yet the entrance into Germany, after passing Nimeguen, was not very promising, being nothing but heath or wood. The woods, however, began to be very pleasant, especially when the inequality of the ground gave us tolerable prospects.

On the evening of Saturday, 10th of September, we arrived at Cleef, and lodged in the park, near the medicinal springs. This is a delightful spot, and from a hill that overhangs the inn we had a most extensive prospect into Germany. At this place we were much entertained with two young Dutchmen, but who, we were informed, were notorious sharpers. They seemed to have some design upon us, but on hearing Lord Shelburne's name, they were visibly embarrassed, and desisted from making any attempt upon us.

The next morning we went through Cleff, and in this country we met a procession of several hundred people walking the town. We just stopped at Sabton to see a curious old church, full of images, and dining at Hoogstraten, we got by dark to Dusseldorff, crossing the Rhine in a *pont volant* just at the town. The roads were very wet and bad.

In the morning we went to see the pictures at the Elector Palatine's palace. Some of them were exquisite, especially a Madona, by Guido. On the road we saw an elegant palace belonging to the elector; and dining at a little inn, on the provisions we carried with us, we arrived at Cologn before it was dark, passing the Rhine just at the city.

In the morning we went to see several churches, but found nothing very remarkable in any of them, besides a picture of the crucifixion of St. Peter, by Rubens. The town is old, ruinous, and disagreeable.

Before dinner we got to Bonn, where we saw the electoral palace, and dined with Mr. Cressner, the English ambassador, the most political character I ever met with, but a very agreeable man. Beyond Cologn I, for the first time, saw vineyards; but from that place to Paris we never lost sight of them long.

On Wednesday we set out early, and got to Coblentz before three o'clock.

The weather was exceedingly wet and unpleasant; otherwise we should have had most delightful travelling.

With this inconvenience it was still singularly fine, and afforded views that were exceedingly striking. We had the Rhine to the left, with hills and rocks covered with vines or woods close to it, the vines intermixed with kidney beans and pumpkins. Sometimes the road was cut in a rock almost perpendicular, the river being below us, and houses above us, with chapels neatly cut in the rock.

Upon our arrival at Coblentz, we waited upon Baron Breidbank, to settle the ceremonial of our visit to the elector, and spent the evening at the inn.

Thursday, we crossed the river to see the citadel, from which, being situated on a high and craggy rock, at the foot of which and close to the river, is the palace, we had a most glorious prospect indeed, seeing the course of the Rhine, with all its windings, to an immense distance, especially up the river; the junction of the Moselle with it, and a fine level of country beyond it, in which was the palace of the elector. Being introduced at court, we dined with the elector, a pleasant looking young man, but said to be a great bigot. The Bishop of Hontheim, a very intelligent man, and one of the company, conducted us to a Carthusian monastery, pleasantly situated on the brow of a hill near the city.

Friday, having crossed the Rhine, our road lay through a very hilly country, and exceedingly romantic. Almost half the day we travelled along the side of a river, which washed the foot of a steep ridge of hills covered with wood, and the side on which we travelled was a rising ground covered with vines. The remainder of the day we travelled through forests and open fields, and arrived at Schwallback just at dark. In the afternoon of this day, Lord Shelburne and I, having walked before the carriage, lost ourselves, which threw me, who was the occasion of it, into great consternation. We imagined the carriage had passed us when it had not.

Sunday, before we set out, we visited the famous spring of Seltzerwater, near this place. The morning was foggy, but it presently cleared up; and when we had reached the top of the hill, we had a most glorious prospect as we travelled along the ridge of it, having the Rhine under us, and an immense tract of country beyond it in view, though frequently interrupted by the trees of the forest through which we passed. We went a little out of our way to see a famous salt and hot spring, but got to Mayence before dinner. This is an agreeable town, and has the air of much politeness. But we made no stay in it, except to see a few churches, and especially a

Carthusian monastery, a little way on our road, out of the town, the cloister of which was finely painted, and arrived at Worms just as it began to be dark.

Sunday, we saw the cathedral, which had been ruined by the French, the Lutheran church, and the town hall, where Luther was examined, now a small garden, and got to Manheim, crossing the Rhine before dinner. Lord Shelburne went to court, escorted by Mr. Dun, while I spent the day at the inn, and hearing a sermon in High Dutch at the Jesuits' church.

Monday, we visited the palace, which is very large and magnificent. We also went to see a collection of models of antique statues, a porcelain warehouse, &c., and reached Landau after the gates were shut, in consequence of Lord Shelburne and I having lost ourselves, and rambled many miles, the carriage having passed us.

Tuesday, we set out early in the morning, and travelling through the rich country of Alsace, got to Strasburgh before night, and time enough to go to the play that evening.

Wednesday, we called upon Professor Spielman, then went to see the bishop's palace and the cathedral, going up the spire, which is said to be the highest in the world, but did not go quite to the top. After dinner we saw the town library, the instruments belonging to the university, and an ingenious electrician called Krafts.

The cultivation of all the tract of country through which we travelled along the Rhine is excellent, especially about Manheim, and in Alsace is most excellent, resembling a rich garden. This look is much favoured by the variety of crops, and the divisions of fields, being often distinguished by rows of vines. All our varieties of corn, turkey wheat, canary seed, hemp, pumpkins, kidney beans, vines, turnips, potatoes, tobacco, and many other things, all intermixed in long and narrow fields, makes a new and curious spectacle to an Englishman. The roads, and also many of the fields, are planted with fruit trees, especially the walnut trees, the fruit of which is useful for making oil.

The soil of this country, and especially of Alsace, is so light that they generally plough with one horse, or cow, which they always yoke by the horns, which was the custom every where in our travels, except in Lorraine, where we saw some oxen yoked as with us. In Lorraine we frequently saw them ploughing with eight horses, and women either holding the plough or driving it. The wheat of Alsace is celebrated. At Strasburgh we had bread of the most exquisitely fine flavour I ever tasted; and at Nancy we were told that they cannot make such in France.

Thursday the 22nd, I rambled into several Lutheran churches, where the ministers were catechising the children and young persons, and among others a class of young women about twenty years of age. After breakfast we left Strasburgh, and dining at Severne, where we saw a magnificent palace of the Archbishop of Strasburgh, we got to Sarreburg before night. From the hills which divide Lorraine from Alsace, we had a noble prospect of all the country to and beyond the Rhine.

Friday, we dined at Luneville, where we saw a curious manufacture of *terre cuite*, and the palace of King Stanislaus, and then reached Nancy before night.

A good deal of the first part of Lorraine is planted with pear-trees, scattered through the fields. The fruit they dry and preserve.

Saturday, went to see Mr. Grenville, about a mile out of town, in a delightful country. We spent the rest of the day in seeing the churches, the square, and the governor's house of this excellent city. In the evening Mr. Grenville brought in the English newspapers.

Sunday, we dined at Metz, after passing a delightful road, with vines on both sides, the valleys well watered and full of cattle. These were the only pastures we saw in all our tour, except in Holland.

Monday, we were detained for want of post horses till after twelve, and spent our time in seeing the churches, the promenade, the arsenal, and a machine for sawing timber. We lodged at Verdun.

Tuesday, we set out early and got to Chalons, where we walked about the town, saw the cathedral, the new town-house, and the promenade.

Wednesday, dined at Rheims, where we saw the cathedral, the treasure belonging to it, and the ancient Roman gate. We lodged at Chalons; the soil poor, but well cultivated.

Thursday, we set out pretty early, and stopping to see a seat of the Duke of Orleans, at Villers Cotevet, a large, but slovenly place, we got to Paris.

In this great capital I cannot say that I was much struck with any thing except the spaciousness and magnificence of the public buildings; and to balance this, I was exceedingly offended with the narrowness, dirt, and stench, of almost all the streets.

Here I spent a month; but though I was far from having any reason to complain of the reception I met with, and saw many truly polite and agreeable people, I cannot say that I saw any person that appeared to be more polite than many that I know in England, especially in the middle ranks of life, where there is, perhaps, more real politeness, as well as more virtue, than in the highest ranks of society.

In general, as far as I can judge, the French are too much taken up with themselves to admit of that minute and benevolent attention to others which is essential to politeness. This appears in nothing more than their continually interrupting one an other in discourse, which they do without the least apology; so that one half of the persons in company are heard talking at the same time. The French are likewise exceedingly deficient in cleanliness. I also happened to be present at such a violent scene of altercation in a private party, as I think would not be suffered in England; and yet the behaviour of the company shewed that they were not much shocked at it. As to mere graciousness of motion and address, as far as I pretend to judge, the English are by no means behind the French with respect to it.

In works of taste in general, and especially in the more ingenious mechanic arts, the French appear to me to be far behind the English, and in nothing could I imagine them superior to the English, or to have any advantage of us with respect to the commodious enjoyment of life, eccept in the arrangement of the parts of a house, which, however, is of late date with them, and which we consult taste in externals too much to have attended to.

Notwithstanding, the French know more of other countries than they used to do, (for before the last war they thought all foreign nations unworthy of their notice), they still have that conceit of themselves, and that contempt of other people, which are the truest marks of barbarism.

The French being debarred from the discussion of politics, by an arbitrary and consequently a jealous government, give very much into a taste for theatrical entertainments; and they seem to have them in greater perfection than with us. But though, for the same reason, many of them apply to literary and philosophical pursuits, they have not attained a decided superiority over other nations in these respects. They shew, however, a spirit and a liberality in these noble studies at which the English ought to blush.

The Memoirs resumed

This little excursion made me more sensible than I should otherwise have been of the benefit of foreign travel, even without the advantage of much conversation with foreigners. The very sight of new countries, new buildings, new customs, &c. and the very hearing of an unintelligible new language, gives new ideas, and tends to enlarge the mind. To me this little time was extremely pleasing, especially as I saw every thing to the greatest advantage, and without any anxiety or trouble, and had an opportunity of seeing and conversing with every person of eminence, where-ever we came; the political characters by his lordship's connexions, and the literary ones by my own. I was soon, however, tired of Paris, and chose to spend my evenings at the hotel, in company with a few literary friends. Fortunately for me, Mr. Magellan being at Paris, at the same time, spent most of the evenings with me; and as I chose to return before his lordship, he accompanied me to London, and made the journey very pleasing to me; he being used to the country, the language, and the manners of it, which I was not. He had seen much of the world, and his conversation during our journey was particularly interesting to me. Indeed, in London, both before and after this time, I always found him very friendly, especially in every thing that related to my philosophical pursuits.

As I was sufficiently apprized of the fact, I did not wonder, as I otherwise should have done, to find all the philosophical persons to whom I was introduced at Paris, unbelievers in Christianity, and even professed Atheists. As I chose on all occasions to appear as a Christian, I was told by some of them, that I was the only person they had ever met with, of whose understanding they had any opinion, who professed to believe Christianity. But on interrogating them on the subject, I soon found that they had given no proper attention to it, and did not really know what Christianity was. This was also the case with a great part of the company that I saw at Lord Shelburne's. But I hope that my always avowing myself to be a Christian, and holding myself ready on all occasions to defend the genuine principles of it, was not without its use. Having conversed so much with unbelievers at home and abroad, I thought I should be able to combat their prejudices with some advantage, and with this view I wrote, while I was with Lord Shelburne, the first part of my 'Letters to a Philosophical Unbeliever', in proof of the doctrines of a God and a providence, and to this I have added during my residence in Birmingham, a second part, in defence of the evidences of Christianity. The first part being replied to by a person who called himself Mr. Hammon, I wrote a reply to his piece, which has hitherto remained unanswered. I am happy to find that this work of mine has done some good, and I hope that in due time it will do more. I can truly say, that the greatest satisfaction I receive from the success of my philosophical pursuits, arises from the weight it may give to my attempts to defend Christianity, and to free it from those corruptions which prevent its reception with philosophical and thinking persons, whose influence with the vulgar, and the unthinking, is very great.

With Lord Shelburne, I saw a great variety of characters; but, of our neighbours in Wiltshire, the person I had the most frequent opportunity of seeing was Dr. Frampton, a clergyman, whose history may serve as a lesson to many. No man, perhaps, was ever better qualified to please in a convivial hour, or had greater talents for conversation and repartee; in consequence of which, though there were several things very disgusting about him, his society was much courted, and many promises of preferment were made to him. To these, notwithstanding his knowledge of the world, and of high life, he gave too much credit; so that he spared no expence to gratify his taste and appetite, until he was universally involved in debt; and though his friends made some efforts to relieve him, he was confined a year in the county prison at a time when his bodily infirmities required the greatest indulgences; and he obtained his release but a short time before his death, on condition of his living on a scanty allowance; the income of his livings (amounting to more than four hundred pounds per annum) being in the hands of his creditors. Such was the end of a man who kept the table in a roar.

Dr. Frampton being a high clergyman, he could not at first conceal his aversion to me, and endeavoured to do me some ill offices. But being a man of letters, and despising the clergy in his neighbourhood, he became at last much attached to me; and in his distresses was satisfied, I believe, that I was one of his most sincere friends. With some great defects he had some considerable virtues, and uncommon abilities, which appeared more particularly in extempore speaking. He always preached without notes, and when, on some occasions, he composed his sermons, he could, if he chose to do it, repeat the whole *verbatim*. He frequently extemporized in verse, in a great variety of measures.

In Lord Shelburne's family, was Lady Arabella Denny, who is well known by her extensive charities. She is (for she is still living) a woman of good understanding, and great piety. She had the care of his lordship's two sons, until they came under the care of Mr. Jervis, who was their tutor during my continuance in the family. His lordship's younger son, who died suddenly, had made astonishing attainments both in knowledge and piety, while very young, far beyond any thing that I had an opportunity of observing in my life.

When I went to his lordship, I had materials for one volume of 'Experiments on Air', which I soon after published, and inscribed to him; and before I left him, I published three volumes more, and had materials for a fourth, which I published immediately on my settling in Birmingham.

He encouraged me in the prosecution of my philosophical inquiries, and allowed me forty pounds per annum for expenses of that kind, and was pleased to see me make experiments to entertain his guests, and especially foreigners.

Notwithstanding the attention that I gave to philosophy in this situation, I did not discontinue my other studies, especially in theology and metaphysics. Here I wrote my 'Miscellaneous Observations relating to Education', and published my 'Lectures on Oratory and Criticism', which I dedicated to Lord Fitzmaurice, Lord Shelburne's eldest son. Here also I published the third and last part of my 'Institutes of Natural and Revealed Religion'; and having in the preface attacked the principles of Dr. Reid, Dr. Beattie, and Dr. Oswald, with respect to their doctrine of *common sense*, which they made to supersede all rational inquiry into the subject of religion, I was led to consider their system in a separate work, which, though written in a manner that I do not entirely approve, has, I hope, upon the whole, been of service to the cause of free inquiry and truth.

In the preface I had expressed my belief of the doctrine of *Philosophical Necessity*, but without any design to pursue the subject, and also my great admiration of Dr. Hartley's theory of the human mind, as indeed I had taken many opportunities of doing before. This led me to publish that part of his 'Observations on Man', which related to the doctrine of association of ideas, detached from the doctrine of vibrations, prefixing 'Three Dissertations', explanatory of his general system. In one of these I expressed some doubt of the immateriality of the sentient principle in man; and the outcry that was made on what I casually expressed on that subject can hardly be imagined. In all the newspapers, and most of the periodical publications, I was represented as an unbeliever in revelation, and no better than an Atheist.

This led me to give the closest attention to the subject, and the consequence was the firmest persuasion that man is wholly material, and that our only prospect of immortality is from the Christian doctrine of a resurrection. I therefore digested my thoughts on the subject, and published my 'Disquisitions relating to Matter and Spirit', also the subjects of 'Socinianism' and 'Necessity', being nearly connected with the doctrine of the materiality of man. I advanced several considerations from the state of opinions in ancient times in favour of the former; and in a separate volume, discussed more at large what related to the latter, dedicating the first volume of this work to Mr. Graham, and the second to Dr. Jebb.

It being probable that this publication would be unpopular, and might be a means of bringing odium on my patron, several attempts were made by his friends, though none by himself, to dissuade me from persisting in it. But being, as I thought, engaged in the cause of important truth, I proceeded without regard to any consequences, assuring them that this publication should not be injurious to his lordship.

In order, however, to proceed with the greatest caution, in a business of such moment, I desired some of my learned friends, and especially Dr. Price, to peruse the work before it was published; and the remarks that he made upon it led to a free and friendly discussion of the several subjects of it, which we afterwards published jointly; and it remains a proof of the possibility of discussing subjects mutually considered as of the greatest importance, with the most perfect good temper, and without the least diminution of frienship. This work I dedicated to our common friend Mr. Lee.

In this situation, I published my 'Harmony of the Gospels', on the idea of the public ministry of Jesus having continued little more than one year, a scheme which I first proposed in the Theological Repository'; and the Bishop of Waterford having in his 'Harmony', published a defence of the common hypothesis, viz, that of its having been three years, I addressed a *letter to him* on the subject, and to this he made a reply in a separate work. The controversy proceeded jointly by us both. Though my side of the question was without any advocates that I know of, and had only been adopted by Mr. Mann, who seemed to have had no followers, there are few persons, I believe, who have attended to our discussion of this subject, who are not satisfied that I have sufficiently proved what I had advanced. This controversy was not finished until after my removal to Birmingham.

Reflecting on the time that I spent with Lord Shelburne, being as a guest in the family, I can truly say that I was not at all fascinated with that mode of life. Instead of looking back upon it with regret, one of the greatest subjects of my present thankfulness is the change of that situation for the one in which I am now placed; and yet I was far from being unhappy there, much less so than those who are born to such a state, and pass all their lives in it. These are generally unhappy from the want of necessary employment; on which account chiefly there appears to be much more happiness in the middle classes of life who are above the fear of want, and yet have a sufficient motive for a constant exertion of their faculties; and who have always some other object besides amusement.

I used to make no scruple of maintaining, that there is not only most virtue, and most happiness, but even most true politeness in the middle classes of life. For in proportion as men pass more of their time in the society of their equals, they get a better established habit of governing their tempers; they attend more to the feelings of others, and are more disposed to accommodate themselves to them. On the other hand, the passions of persons in higher life, having been less controlled, are more apt to be inflamed; the idea of their rank and superiority to others, seldom quits them; and though they are in the habit of concealing their feelings, and disguising their passions, it is not always so well done, but that persons of ordinary discernment may perceive what they inwardly suffer. On this account, they are really entitled to compassion, it being the almost unavoidable consequence of their education and mode of life. But when the mind is not hurt in such a situation, when a person born to affluence can lose sight of himself, and truly feel and act for others, the character is so godlike, as shews that this inequality of condition is not without its use. Like the general discipline of life, it is for the present lost on the great mass, but on a few it produces what no other state of things could do.

The greatest part of the time that I spent with Lord Shelburne, I passed with much satisfaction, his lordship always behaving to me with uniform politeness, and his guests with respect. But about two years before I left him, I perceived evident marks of dissatisfaction, though I never understood the cause of it; and until that time he had been even lavish on all occasions in expressing his satisfaction in my society, to our common friends. When I left him, I asked him whether he had any fault to find with my conduct, and he said *none*. At length, however, he intimated to Dr. Price, that he wished to give me an establishment in Ireland, where he had large property. This gave me an opportunity of acquainting him, that if he chose to dissolve the connection, it should be on the terms expressed in the writings, which we mutually signed when it was formed, in consequence of which I should be intitled to an annuity of an hundred and fifty pounds, and then I would provide for myself, and to this he readily acceded. He told Dr. Price that he wished our separation to be amicable, and I assured him that nothing should be wanting on my part to make it truly so. Accordingly, I expected that he would receive my visits when I should be occasionally in London, but he declined them.

However, when I had been some years settled at Birmingham, he sent an especial messenger, and common friend, to engage me again in his service, having, as that friend assured me, a deep sense of the loss of Lord Ashburton (Mr. Dunning) by death, and of Colonel Carre, by his becoming almost blind, and his want of some able and faithful friend, such as he had experienced in me; with other expressions more flattering than those. I did not chuse, however, on any consideration, to leave the very eligible situation in which I now am, but expressed my readiness to do him any service in my power. His lordship's enemies have insinuated that he was not punctual in the payment of my annuity; but the contrary is true: hitherto nothing could have been more punctual, and I have no reason to suppose that it will ever be otherwise.

At Calne, I had another son born to me, whom at Lord Shelburne's request, I called Henry.

It was at the time of my leaving Lord Shelburne, that I found the great value of Mr. and Mrs. Lindsey's friendship, in such a manner as I certainly had no expectation of when our acquaintance commenced; especially by their introducing me to the notice of Mrs. Rayner, one of his hearers and most zealous friends.

Notwithstanding my allowance from Lord Shelburne was larger than that which I had at Leeds, yet my family growing up, and my expenses, on this and other accounts, increasing more than in proportion, I was barely able to support my removal. But my situation being intimated to Mrs. Rayner, besides smaller sums, with which she occasionally assisted me, she gave me an hundred guineas to defray the expence of my removal and deposited with Mrs. Lindsey, which she soon after gave up to me four hundred guineas, and to this day has never failed giving me every year marks of her friendship. Her's is, indeed, I seriously think, one of the first Christian characters that I was ever acquainted with, having a cultivated comprehensive mind, equal to any subject of theology or metaphysics, intrepid in the cause of truth, and most rationally pious.

Spending so much of my time in London, was the means of increasing my intimacy with both Mr. Lindsey and Mr. Lee, our common friend; who amidst the bustle of politics, always preserved his attachment to theology, and the cause of truth. The Sunday I always spent with Mr. Lindsey, attending the service of his chapel, and sometimes officiating for him; and with him and Mrs. Lindsey I generally spent the evening of that day at Mr. Lee's, who then admitted no other company, and seldom have I enjoyed society with more relish.

My winter's residence in London was the means of improving my acquaintance with Dr. Franklin. I was seldom many days without seeing him, and being members of the same club, we constantly returned together. The difference with America breaking out at this time, our conversation was chiefly of a political nature, and I can bear witness that he was so far from promoting, as was generally supposed, that he took every method in his power to prevent, a rupture between the two countries. He urged so much the doctrine of forbearance, that for some time he was unpopular with the Americans on that account, as too much a friend to Great Britain. His advice to them was to bear every thing for the present as they were sure in time to out-grow all their grievances; as it could not be in the power of the country to oppress them long.

He dreaded the war, and often said that, if the difference should come to an open rupture, it would be a war of *ten years*, and he should not live to see the end of it. In reality the war lasted nearly eight years, but he did live to see the happy termination of it. That the issue would be favourable to America, he never doubted. The English, he used to say, may take all our great towns, but that will not give them possession of the country. The last day that he spent in England, having given out that he should leave London the day before, we passed together, without any other company; and much of the time was employed in reading American newspapers, especially accounts of the reception which the 'Boston Port Bill', met with in America; and as he read the addresses to the inhabitants of Boston, from the places in the neighbourhood, the tears trickled down his cheeks.

It is much to be lamented, that a man of Dr. Franklin's general good character, and great influence, should have been an unbeliever in Christianity, and also have done so much as he did to make others unbelievers. To me, however, he acknowledged that he had not given so much attention as he ought to have done, to the evidences of Christianity, and desired me to recommend to him a few treatises on the subject, such as I thought most deserving of his motive, but not of great length, promising to read them, and give me his sentiments on them. Accordingly, I recommended to him Hartley's evidence of Christianity in his observations on man, and what I had then written on the subject in my 'Institutes of Natural and Revealed Religion'. But the American war breaking out soon after, I do not believe that he ever found himself sufficiently at leisure for the discussion. I have kept up a correspondence with him occasionally, ever since, and three of his letters to me were, with his consent, published in his miscellaneous works, in quarto. The first of them written, immediately on his landing in America, is very striking.

About three years before the dissolution of my connexion with Lord Shelburne, Dr. Fothergill, with whom I had always lived on terms of much intimacy, having observed, as he said, that many of my experiments had not been carried to their proper extent on account of the expence that would have attended them, proposed to me a subscription from himself and some of his friends, to supply me with whatever sums I should want for that purpose, and named a hundred pounds per annum. This large subscription I declined, lest the discovery of it (by the use that I should, of course, make of it) should give umbrage to Lord Shelburne, but I consented to accept of forty pounds per annum, which from that time he regularly paid me, from the contribution of himself, Sir Theodore Jansen, Mr. Constable, and Sir George Saville.

On my leaving Lord Shelburne, which was attended with the loss of one half of my income, Dr. Fothergill proposed an enlargement of my allowance for my experiments, and likewise for my maintenance, without being under the necessity of giving my time to pupils, which I must otherwise have done. And, considering the generosity with which this voluntary offer was made by persons who could well afford it, and who thought me qualified to serve the interests of science, I thought it right to accept of it: and I preferred it to any pension from the court, offers of which were more than once made by persons who thought they could have procured one for me.

As it was my wish to do what might be in my power to shew my gratitude to my friends and benefactors that suggested the idea of writing these memoirs, I shall subjoin a list of their names. Some of the subscriptions were made with a view to defray the expence of my experiments only; but the greater part of the subscribers were persons who were equally friends to my theological studies.

The persons who made me this regular annual allowance, were Dr. Watson and his son, Mr. Wedgwood, Mr. Moseley, Mr. S. Salte, Mr. Jeffries, Mr. Radcliffe, Mr. Reminton, Mr. Strutt, of Derby; Mr. Shore, Mr. Reynolds, of Paxton; Messrs. Galton, father and son, and the Rev. Mr. Simpson.

Besides the persons whose names appear in this list, as regular subscribers, there were other persons who, without chusing to be known as such, contributed no less to my support, and some considerably more.

My chief benefactress was Mrs. Rayner, and next to her Dr. Heberden, equally distinguished for his love of religious truth, and his zeal to promote science. Such also is the character of Mr. Tayleur, of Shrewsbury, who has at different times remitted me considerable sums, chiefly to defray the expences incurred by my theological inquiries and publications.

Mr. Parker, of Fleet-Street, very generously supplied me with every instrument that I wanted in glass, particularly a capital burning lens, sixteen inches in diameter. All his benefactions in this way would have amounted to a considerable sum. Mr. Wedgwood also, besides his annual benefaction, supplied me with every thing that I wanted made of pottery, such as retorts, tubes, &c. which the account of my experiments will shew to have been of great use to me.

On my removal to Birmingham, commenced my intimacy with Mr. William Russell, whose public spirit, and zeal in every good cause, can hardly be exceeded. My obligations to him were various and constant, so as not to be estimated by sums of money. At his proposal I doubt not, some of the heads of the congregation made me a present of two hundred pounds, to assist me in my theological publications.

Mr. Lee shewed himself particularly my friend, at the time that I left Lord Shelburne, assisting me in the difficulties with which I was then pressed, and continuing to befriend me afterwards by seasonable benefactions. By him it was hinted to me during the administration of Lord Rockingham, with whom he had great influence, that I might have a pension from the government, to assist in defraying the expense of my experiments. Another hint of the same kind was given me in the beginning of Mr. Pitt's administration, by a bishop, in whose power it was to have procured it from him. But in both cases I declined the overture, wishing to preserve myself indipendent of every thing connected with the court, and preferring the assistance of generous and opulent individuals, lovers of science, and also lovers of liberty. Without assistance I could not have carried on my experiments except on a very small scale, and under great disadvantages.

Mr. Galton, before I had any opportunity of being personally acquainted with him, had, on the death of Dr. Fothergill, taken up his subscription. His son did the same, and the friendship of the latter has added much to the happiness of my situation here.* Seldom, if ever, have I known two persons of such cultivated minds, pleasing manners and liberal dispositions as he and Mrs. Galton. The latter had the greatest attachment imaginable to my wife.

Mr. Salte was zealous in promoting the subscriptions to my experiments, and moreover proposed to take one of my sons as an apprentice, without any fee. But my brother-in-law making the same offer, I gave it the

---

* Birmingham.

preference. Mr. Wedgwood, who has distinguished himself by his application to philosophical pursuits, as well as by his great success in the improvements of his manufactory, was very zealous to serve me, and urged me to accept of a much larger allowance than I chose.

The favours that I received from my two brothers-in-law, deserve my most grateful acknowledgements. They acted the part of kind and generous relations, especially at the time when I most wanted assistance. It was in consequence of Mr. John Wilkinson's proposal, who wished to have us nearer to him, that, being undetermined where to settle, I fixed upon Birmingham, where he soon provided a house for me.

My apology for accepting of these large benefactions is, that besides the great expense of my philosophical and even my theological studies, and the education of three sons and a daughter, the reputation I had, justly or unjustly acquired, brought on me a train of expences not easy to describe, to avoid, or to estimate; so that without so much as keeping a horse, (which the kindness of Mr. Russel made unnecessary) the expense of housekeeping, &c. was more than double the amount of any regular income that I had.

I consider my settlement at Birmingham as the happiest event in my life, being highly favourable to every object I had in view philosophical or theological. In the former respect, I had the convenience of good workmen of every kind, and the society of persons eminent for their knowledge of chemistry, particularly Mr. Watt, Mr. Keir, and Dr. Withering. These with Mr. Boulton, and Dr. Darwin, who soon left us, by removing from Lichfield to Derby, Mr. Galton, and afterwards Mr. Johnson, of Kenelworth, and myself, dined together every month, calling ourselves the *Lunar Society*, because the time of our meeting was near the full moon.

With respect to theology, I had the society of Mr. Hawkes, Mr. Blyth, and Mr. Scholefield, and his assistant Mr. Coates, and, while he lived, Mr. Palmer, before of Macclesfield. We met and drank tea together every fortnight. At this meeting we read all the papers that were sent for the 'Theological Repository', which I revived some time after my coming hither, and in general our conversation was of the same cast as that with my fellow tutors at Warrington.

Within a quarter of a year of my coming to reside at Birmingham, Mr. Hawkes resigned, and I had an unanimous invitation to succeed him, as colleague with Mr. Blyth, a man of a truly Christian temper. The congregation we serve is the most liberal, I believe, of any in England; and to this freedom the unwearied labours of Mr. Bourne had eminently contributed.

With this congregation I greatly improved my plan of catechizing and lecturing, and my classes have been well attended. I have also introduced the custom of expounding the scriptures as I read them, which I had never done before, but which I would earnestly recommend to all ministers. My time being much taken up with my philosophical and other studies, I agreed with the congregation to leave the business of baptizing, and visiting the sick, to Mr. Blyth, and to confine my services to the Sundays. I have been minister here between seven and eight years, without any interruption of my happiness; and for this I am sensible I am in a great measure indebted to the friendship of Mr. Russell.

Here I have never long intermitted my philosophical pursuits, and I have published two volumes of experiments, besides communications to the Royal Society.

In theology I have completed my friendly controversy with the Bishop of Waterford, on the duration of Christ's ministry, I have published a variety of single sermons, which, with the addition of a few others, I have lately collected and published in one volume, and I am now engaged in a controversy of great extent, and which promises to be of considerable consequence, relating to the person of Christ.

This was occasioned by my 'History of the Corruptions of Christianity', which I composed and published presently after my settlement at Birmingham, the first section of which being rudely attacked in the 'Monthly Review', then by Dr. Horsley, and afterwards by Mr. Howes, and other particular opponents, I undertook to collect from the original writers the state of opinions on the subject in the age succeeding that of the apostles, and I have published the result of my investigation in my 'History of Early Opinions concerning Jesus Christ', in four volumes octavo. This work has brought me more antagonists, and I now write a pamphlet annually in defence of the Unitarian doctrine against all my opponents.

My only Arian antagonist is Dr. Price, with whom the discussion of the question has proceeded with perfect amity. But no Arian has as yet appeared upon the ground to which I wish to confine the controversy, viz. the state of opinions in the primitive times, as one means of collecting what was the doctrine of the apostles, and the true sense of scripture on the subject.

Some years ago I resumed the 'Theological Repository', in which I first advanced my objections to the doctrine of the miraculous conception of Jesus, and his natural fallibility and peccability. These opinions gave at first great alarm, even to my best friends; but that is now in a great measure subsided. For want of sufficient sale, I shall be obliged to discontinue this 'Repository' for some time.

At present I thank God I can say that my prospects are better than they have ever been before, and my own health, and that of my wife, better established, and my hopes as to the dispositions and future settlement of my children satisfactory.

I shall now close this account of myself with some observations of a general nature, but chiefly an account of those circumstances for which I have more particular reason to be thankful to that good Being who has brought me hitherto, and to whom I trust I habitually ascribe whatever my partial friends think the world indebted to me for.

Not to enlarge again on what has been mentioned already, on the fundamental blessings of a religious and liberal education, I have particular reason to be thankful for a happy temperament of body and mind, both derived from my parents. My father, grandmother, and several branches of the family, were remarkably healthy, and long lived; and though my constitution has been far from robust, and was much injured by a consumptive tendency, or rather an ulcer in my lungs, the consequence of improper conduct of myself when I was at school, (being often violently heated with exercise, and as often imprudently chilled by bathing, &c) from which with great difficulty I recovered, it has been excellently adapted to that studious life which has fallen to my lot.

I have never been subject to head-aches, or any other complaints that are peculiarly unfavourable to study. I have never found myself less disposed, or less qualified, for mental exertions of any kind at one time of the day more than another; but all seasons have been equal to me, early or late, before dinner or after, &c. And so far have I been from suffering by my application to study, (which however has never been so close or intense as some have imagined) that I have found my health improving from the age of eighteen to the present time; and never have I found myself more free from any disorder, than at present. I must, however, except a short time preceding and following my leaving Lord Shelburne, when I laboured under a bilious complaint, in which I was troubled with gall stones, which sometimes gave me exquisite pain. But by confining myself to a vegetable diet, I perfectly recovered; and I have now been so long free from the disorder, that I am under no apprehension of its return.

It has been a singular happiness to me, and a proof, I believe, of a radically good constitution, that I have always slept well, and have awaked with my faculties perfectly vigorous without any disposition to drowsiness.

Also, whenever I have been fatigued with any kind of exertion, I could at any time sit down and sleep; and whatever cause of anxiety I may have had, I have almost always lost sight of it when I have got to bed; and I have generally fallen asleep as soon as I have been warm.*

I even think it an advantage to me, and am truly thankful for it, that my health received the check that it did, when I was young; since a muscular habit from high health, and strong spirits, are not, I think, in general accompanied with that sensibility of mind, which is both favourable to piety, and to speculative pursuits.†

To a fundamentally good constitution of body, and the being who gave it me, I owe an even cheerfulness of temper, which has had but a few interruptions. This I inherit from my father, who had uniformly better spirits than any man that I ever knew, and by this means was as happy towards the close of life, when reduced to poverty, and dependent upon others, as in his best days; and who, I am confident, would not have been unhappy, as I have frequently heard him say, in a workhouse.

Though my readers will easily suppose that, in the course of a life so full of vicissitude as mine has been, many things must have occurred to mortify and discompose me, nothing has ever depressed my mind beyond a very short period. My spirits have never failed to recover their natural level, and I have frequently observed, and at first with some surprise, that the most perfect satisfaction I have ever felt has been a day or two after an event that afflicted me the most, and without any change having taken place in the state of things. Having found this to be the case after many of my troubles, the persuasion that it *would* be so, after a new cause of uneasiness, has never failed to lessen the effect of its first impression, and together with my firm belief of the doctrine of necessity, and (consequently that of every thing being ordered for the best) has contributed to that degree of composure which I have enjoyed through life, so that I have always considered myself as one of the happiest of men.

When I was a young author, (though I did not publish any thing until I was about thirty) strictures on my writings gave me some disturbance, though I believe even the less than they do most others; but after some

---

* My father was an early riser. He never slept more than six hours. He said he did not remember having lost a whole night's sleep but once, though when awake he often had to suffer much from pain and sickness as well as from other circumstances of a very afflictive nature.

† Though not a muscular man, he went through great exertion at various times of his life with activity. He walked very firmly and expeditiously.

time, things of that kind hardly affected me at all, and on this account I may be said to have been well formed for public controversy.* But what has always made me easy in any controversy in which I have been engaged, has been my fixed resolution frankly to acknowledge any mistake that I perceive I had fallen into. That I have never been in the least backward to do this in matters of philosophy, can never be denied.

As I have not failed to attend to the phenomena of my own mind, as well as to those of other parts of nature, I have not been insensible of some great defects, as well as some advantages, attending its constitution; having from an early period been subject to a most humbling failure of recollection, so that I have sometimes lost all ideas of both persons and things, that I have been conversant with. I have so completely forgotten what I have myself published, that in reading my own writings, what I find in them often appears perfectly new to me, and I have more than once made experiments, the results of which had been published by me.

I shall particularly mention one fact of this kind, as it alarmed me much at the time, as a symptom of all my mental powers totally failing me, until I was relieved by the recollection of things of a similar nature having happened to me before. When I was composing the 'Dissertations', which are prefixed to my 'Harmony of the Gospels', I had to ascertain something which had been the subject of much discussion, relating to the Jewish passover, (I have now forgotten what it was) and for that purpose had to consult and compare several writers. This I accordingly did, and digested the result in a compass of a few paragraphs, which I wrote in short hand. But having mislaid the paper, and my attention having been drawn off to other things, in the space of a fortnight, I did the same thing over again; and should never have discovered that I had done it twice, if, after the second paper was transcribed for the press, I had not accidentally found the former, which I viewed with a degree of terror.

Apprized of this defect, I never fail to note down, as soon as possible, every thing that I wish not to forget. The same failing has led me to devise, and have recourse to, a variety of mechanical expedients to secure and arrange my thoughts, which have been of the greatest use to me in the

---

* Though Dr. Priestley has been considered as fond of controversy, and that his chief delight consisted in it, yet it is far from being true. He was more frequently the defendant than the assailant. His controversies, as far as it depended upon himself, were carried on with temper and decency. He was never malicious, nor even sarcastic, or indignant, unless provoked.

composition of large and complex works; and what has excited the wonder of some of my readers would only have made them smile if they had seen me at work. But by simple and mechanical methods one man shall do that in a month, which shall cost another, of equal ability, whole years to execute. This methodical arrangement of a large work, is greatly facilitated by mechanical methods, and nothing contributes more to the perspicuity of a large work, than a good arrangement of its parts.

What I have known with respect to myself, has tended much to lessen both my admiration, and my contempt, of others. Could we have entered into the mind of Sir Isaac Newton, and have traced all the steps by which he produced his great works, we might see nothing very extraordinary in the process. And great powers with respect to some things are generally attended with great defects in others; and these may not appear in a man's writings. For this reason, it seldom happens but that our admiration of philosophers and writers is lessened by a personal knowledge of them.

As great excellencies are often balanced by great, though not apparent defects, so great and apparent defects are often accompanied by great though not apparent excellencies. Thus my defect in point of recollection, which may be owing to a want of sufficient coherence in the association of ideas formerly impressed, may arise from a mental constitution more favourable to new associations; so that what I have lost with respect to memory, may have been compensated by what is called invention, or new and original combinations of ideas. This is a subject that deserves attention, as well as every thing else that relates to the affections of the mind.

Though I have often composed much in a little time, it by no means follows that I could have done much in a given time. For whenever I have done much business, in a short time, it has always been with the idea of having time more than sufficient to do it in; so that I have always felt myself at ease, and I could have done nothing, as many can, if I had been hurried.

Knowing the necessity of this state of my mind to the dispatch of business, I have never put off any thing to the last moment; and instead of doing that on the morrow which ought to be done to-day, I have often blamed myself for doing to-day, what had better have been put off until to-morrow; precipitancy being more my fault than procrastination.

It has been a great advantage to me, that I have never been under the necessity of retiring from company in order to compose any thing. Being fond of domestic life, I got a habit of writing on any subject by the parlour fire, with my wife and children about me, and occasionally talking to them, without experiencing any inconvenience from such interruptions. Nothing but reading, or speaking without interruption, has been any obstruction to me. For I could not help attending (as some can) when others spoke in my hearing. Those are useful habits, which studious persons in general might acquire, if they would; and many persons greatly distress themselves, and others, by the idea that they can do nothing except in perfect solitude or silence.

Another great subject of my thankfulness to a good providence, is my perfect freedom from any embarrassment in my circumstances, so that, without any anxiety on the subject, my supplies have always been equal to my wants; and now that my expenses are increased to a degree that I had no conception of some years ago, I am a richer man than I was, and without laying myself out for the purpose. What is more, this indifference about an increase of fortune has been the means of attaining it. When I began my experiments, I expended on them all the money I could possibly raise, carried on by my ardour in philosophical investigations, and entirely regardless of consequences, except so far as never to contract any debt; and if this had been without success, my imprudence would have been manifest. But having succeeded, I was in time more than indemnified for all that I had expended.

My theological studies, especially those which made it necessary for me to consult the Christian fathers, &c. have also been expensive to me. But I have found my theological friends even more liberal than my philosophical ones, and all beyond my expectations.

In reflecting on my past life, I have often thought of two sayings of Jacob. When he had lost one of his sons, and thought of other things that were afflictions to him, he said, 'all these things are against me'; at the same time that they were in reality making for him. So the impediment in my speech, and the difficulties of my situation at Needham, I now see as much cause to be thankful for, as for the most brilliant scenes in my life.

I have also applied to myself what Jacob said on his return from Padan Aram. 'With my staff I went over this Jordan, and now I am become two bands'; when I consider how little I carried with me to Needham and Nantwich, how much more I had to carry to Warrington, how much more still to Leeds, how much more than that to Calne, and then to Birmingham.

Yet, frequently as I have changed my situation, and always for the better, I can truly say that I never wished for any change on my own account. I should have been contented even at Needham, if I could have been unmolested, and had bare necessaries. This freedom from anxiety was remarkable in my father, and therefore is in a manner hereditary to me; but it has been much increased by reflection; having frequently observed, especially with respect to Christian ministers, how often it has contributed to embitter their lives, without being of any use to them. Some attention to the improvement of a man's circumstances is, no doubt, right, because no man can tell what occasion he may have for money, especially if he have children, and therefore, I do not recommend my example to others. But I am thankful to that good providence, which always took more care of me than ever I took of myself.

Hitherto I have had great reason to be thankful with respect to my children, as they have a prospect of enjoying a good share of health, and a sufficient capacity for performing the duties of their stations. They have also good dispositions, and as much as could be expected at their age, a sense of religion. But as I hope they will live to see this work, I say the less on this subject, and I hope they will consider what I say in their favour, as an incitement to exert themselves to act a Christian and useful part in life; that the care that I and their mother have taken of their instruction, may not be lost upon them, and that they may secure a happy meeting with us in a better world.

I esteem it a singular happiness to have lived in an age and country, in which I have been at full liberty both to investigate, and by preaching and writing to propagate, religious truth; that though the freedom I have used for this purpose was for some time disadvantageous to me, it was not long so, and that my present situation is such that I can with the greatest openness urge whatever appears to me to be the truth of the gospel, and not only without giving the least offence, but with the entire approbation of those with whom I am particularly connected.

As to the dislike which I have drawn upon myself by my writings, whether that of the Calvinistic party, in or out of the church of England; those who rank with rational Dissenters, (but who have been exceedingly offended at my carrying my inquiries farther than they wished any person to do) or whether they be unbelievers, I am thankful that it gives less disturbance to me than it does to themselves; and that their dislike is much more than compensated by the cordial esteem and approbation of my conduct by a few, whose minds are congenial to my own, and especially that the number of such persons increases.

Birmingham, 1787.

*A continuation of the Memoirs, written at Northumberland, in
America, in the beginning of the year 1795.*

When I wrote the preceeding part of these Memoirs, I was happy, as must
have appeared in the course of them, in the prospect of spending the
remainder of my life at Birmingham, where I had every advantage for
pursuing my studies, both philosophical and theological; but it pleased the
sovereign disposer of all things to appoint for me other removals, and the
manner in which they were brought about, were more painful to me than
the removals themselves. I am far, however, from questioning the wisdom
or the goodness of the appointments respecting myself or others.

To resume the account of my pursuits, where the former part of the
Memoirs left it, I must observe that, in the prosecution of my *experiments*, I
was led to maintain the doctrine of phlogiston against Mr. Lavoisier, and
other chemists in France, whose opinions were adopted not only by almost
all the philosophers of that country, but by those in England and Scotland
also. My friends, however, of the lunar society, were never satisfied with
the anti-phlogistic doctrine. My experiments and observations on this
subject, were published in various papers in the 'Philosophical Transactions'. At Birmingham I also published a new edition of my publications
on the subject of *air*, and others connected with it, reducing the six volumes
to three, which, with his consent, I dedicated to the Prince of Wales.

In theology, I continued my 'Defences of Unitarianism', until it
appeared to myself and my friends, that my antagonists produced nothing
to which it was of any consequence to reply. But I did not, as I had
proposed, publish any address to the bishops, or to the legislature, on the
subject. The former I wrote but did not publish. I left it, however, in the
hands of Mr. Belsham, when I came to America, that he might dispose of
it as he should think proper.

The pains that I took to ascertain the state of early opinions concerning
Jesus Christ, and the great misapprehensions I perceived in all the
ecclesiastical historians, led me to undertake a 'General History of the
Christian Church to the Fall of the Western Empire', which accordingly I
wrote in two volumes octavo, and dedicated to Mr. Shore. This work I mean
to continue.

At Birmingham I wrote the 'Second Part' of my 'Letters to a Philosophical Unbeliever', and dedicated the whole to Mr. Tayleur, of
Shrewsbury, who had afforded the most material assistance in the

publication of many of my theological works, without which, the sale being inconsiderable, I should not have been able to publish them at all.

Before I left Birmingham I preached a funeral sermon for my friend, Dr. Price, and another for Mr. Robinson, of Cambridge, who died with us on a visit to preach our annual charity school sermon. I also preached the last annual sermon to the friends of the college at Hackney. All these three sermons were published.

About two years before I left Birmingham, the question about the 'Test Act', was much agitated both in and out of parliament. This, however, was altogether without any concurrence of mine. I only delivered, and published, a sermon, on the 5th of November, 1789, recommending the most peaceable method of pursuing our object. Mr. Madan, however, the most respectable clergyman in the town, preaching and publishing a very inflammatory sermon on the subject, inveighing in the bitterest manner against the Dissenters in general, and myself in particular, I addressed a number of 'Familiar Letters to the Inhabitants of Birmingham', in our defence. This produced a reply from him, and other letters from me. All mine were written in an ironical and rather a pleasant manner, and in some of the last of them I introduced a farther reply to Mr. Burn, another clergyman in Birmingham, who had addressed to me 'Letters on the Infallibility of the Testimony of the Apostles, concerning the Person of Christ', after replying to his first set of letters in a separate publication.

From these small pieces, I was far from expecting any serious consequences. But the dissenters in general being very obnoxious to the court, and it being imagined, though without any reason, that I had been the chief promoter of the measures which gave them offence, the clergy, not only in Birmingham, but through all England, seemed to make it their business, by writing in the public papers, by preaching and other methods, to inflame the minds of the people against me. And on occasion of the celebration of the anniversary of the French Revolution, on July 14, 1791, by several of my friends, but with which I had little to do, a mob encouraged by some persons in power, first burned the meeting-house in which I preached, then another meeting-house in the town, and then my dwelling-house, demolishing my library, apparatus, and, as far as they could, every thing belonging to me. They also burned, or much damaged, the houses of many dissenters, chiefly my friends; the particulars of which I need not recite, as they will be found in two 'Appeals', which I published on the subject, written presently after the riots.

Being in some personal danger on this occasion, I went to London; and

E

so violent was the spirit of party which then prevailed, that I believe I could hardly have been safe in any other place.

There, however, I was perfectly so, though I continued to be an object of troublesome attention until I left the country altogether. It shewed no small degree of courage and friendship in Mr. William Vaughan, to receive me into his house, and also in Mr. Salte, with whom I spent a month at Tottenham. But it shewed more in Dr. Price's congregation, at Hackney, to invite me to succeed him, which they did, though not unanimously, some time after my arrival in London.

In this situation I found myself as happy as I had been at Birmingham; and contrary to general expectation, I opened my lectures to young persons with great success, being attended by many from London; and though I lost some of the hearers, I left the congregation in a better situation than that in which I found it.

On the whole, I spent my time even more happily at Hackney than ever I had done before; having every advantage for my philosophical and theological studies, in some respect superior to what I had enjoyed at Birmingham, especially from my easy access to Mr. Lindsey, and my frequent intercourse with Mr. Belsham, professor of divinity in the new College, near which I lived. Never, on this side the grave, do I expect to enjoy myself so much as I did by the fire-side of Mr. Lindsey, conversing with him and Mrs. Lindsey on theological and other subjects, or in my frequent walks with Mr. Belsham, whose views of most important subjects were, like Mr. Lindsey's the same as my own.

I found, however, my society much restricted with respect to my philosophical acquaintance; most of the members of the Royal Society shunning me on account of my religious or political opinions, so that I at length withdrew myself from them, and gave my reasons for doing so in the preface to my 'Observations and Experiments on the Generation of Air from Water', which I published in Hackney. For, with the assistance of my friends, I had in a great measure replaced my apparatus, and had resumed my experiments, though after the loss of nearly two years.

Living in the neighbourhood of the New College, I voluntarily undertook to deliver the lectures to the pupils on the subject of 'History and General Policy', which I had composed at Warrington, and also on 'Experimental Philosophy and Chemistry', the 'Heads' of which I drew up for this purpose, and afterwards published. In being useful to this institution, I found a source of considerable satisfaction to myself. Indeed, I have always had a high degree of enjoyment in lecturing to young persons, though more on theological subjects than on any other.

After the riots in Birmingham, I wrote 'An Appeal to the Public' on the subject, and that being replied to by the clergy of the place, I wrote a 'Second Part', to which, though they had pledged themselves to do it, they made no reply; so that, in fact, the criminality of the magistrates, and other principal high-churchmen, at Birmingham, in promoting the riot, remains acknowledged. Indeed, many circumstances which have appeared since that time, shew that the friends of the court, if not the prime ministers themselves, were the favourers of that riot; having, no doubt, thought to intimidate the friends of liberty by the measure.

To my appeal I subjoined various 'Addresses' that were sent to me from several descriptions of persons in England, and abroad; and from them I will not deny that I received much satisfaction, as it appeared that the friends of liberty, civil and religious, were of opinion that I was a sufferer in that cause. From France I received a considerable number of addresses; and when the present *National Convention* was called, I was invited by many of the departments to be a member of it. But I thought myself more usefully employed at home, and that I was but ill qualified for a business which required knowledge which none but a native of the country could possess; and therefore declined the honour that was proposed to me.

But no addresses gave me so much satisfaction as those from my late congregation, and especially of the young persons belonging to it, who had attended my lectures. They are a standing testimony of the zeal and fidelity with which I did my duty with respect to them, and which I value highly.

Besides congratulatory addresses, I received much pecuniary assistance from various persons, and bodies of men, which more than compensated for my pecuniary losses, though what was awarded me at the assizes fell two thousand pounds short of them. But my brother-in-law, Mr. John Wilkinson from whom I had not at that time any expectation, in consequence of my son's leaving his employment, was the most generous on the occasion. Without any solicitation he immediately sent me five hundred pounds, which he had deposited in the French funds, and until that be productive, he allows me two hundred pounds per annum.

After the riots, I published my 'Letters to the Swedenborgian Society', which I had composed and prepared for the press just before.

Mr. Wakefield living in the neighbourhood of the college, and publishing at this time his objections to *public worship,* they made a great impression on many of our young men, and in his preface he reflected much on the character of Dr. Price. On both those accounts I thought myself called upon to reply to him, which I did in a series of 'Letters to a Young Man'. Though he made several angry replies, I never noticed any of them. In this situation I also answered Mr. Evanson's 'Observations on the dissonance of the Evangelists, in a Second Set of Letters to a Young Man'. He also replied to me, but I was satisfied with what I had done, and did not continue the controversy.

Besides the 'Sermon' which I delivered on my acceptance of the invitation to the meeting at Hackney, in the preface to which I gave a detailed account of my *systems of catechizing,* I published two 'Fast Sermons', for the years 1793 and 1794, in the latter of which I gave my ideas of ancient prophecies, compared with the then state of Europe, and in the preface to it I gave an account of my reasons for leaving the country. I also published a 'Farewell Sermon'.

But the most important of my publications in this situation, were a series of 'Letters to the Philosophers and Politicians of France, on the Subject of Religion'. I thought that the light in which I then stood in that country, gave me some advantage in my attempts to enforce the evidence of natural and revealed religion. I also published a set of 'Sermons on the Evidences of Revelation', which I first delivered by public notice, and the delivery of which was attended by great numbers. They were printed just before I left England.

As the reasons for this step in my conduct are given at large in the preface to my 'Fast Sermon', I shall not dwell upon them here. The bigotry of the country in general made it impossible for me to place my sons in it to any advantage. William had been some time in France, and on the breaking out of the troubles in that country, he had embarked for America, where his two brothers met him. My own situation, if not hazardous, was become unpleasant, so that I thought my removal would be of more service to the cause of truth than my longer stay in England. At length, therefore, with the approbation of all my friends, without exception, but with great reluctance on my own part, I came to that resolution; I being at a time of life in which I could not expect much satisfaction as to friends and society, comparable to that which I left, in which the resumption of my philosophical pursuits must be attended with great disadvantage, and in which success, in my still more favourite pursuit, the propagation of Unitarianism, was still more uncertain. It was also painful to me to leave my daughter, Mr. Finch having the greatest aversion to leave his relations and friends in England.

At the time of my leaving England, my son, in conjunction with Mr. Cooper and other emigrants, had a scheme for a large settlement for the friends of liberty in general, near the head of Susquehanna, in Pennsylvania. And taking it for granted that it would be carried into effect, after landing at New York I went to Philadelphia, and thence came to Northumberland, a town the nearest to the proposed settlement, thinking to reside there until some progress had been made in it. The settlement was given up; but being here, and my wife and myself liking the place, I have determined to take up my residence here, though subject to many disadvantages. Philadelphia was excessively expensive, and this comparatively a cheap place; and my sons settling in the neighbourhood will be less exposed to temptation, and more likely to form habits of sobriety and industry. They will also be settled at much less expence than in or near a large town. We hope, after some time, to be joined by a few of our friends from England, that a readier communication will be opened with Philadelphia, and that the place will improve, and become more eligible in other respects.

When I was at sea, I wrote some 'Observations on the Cause of the present Prevalence of Infidelity', which I published, and prefixed to a new edition of the 'Letters to the Philosophers and Politicians of France'. I have also published my 'Fast and Farewell Sermons', and my 'Small Tracts', in defence of Unitarianism; also a 'Continuation of those Letters', and a 'Third Part of Letters to a Philosophical Unbeliever', in answer to Mr. Paine's 'Age of Reason'.

The observations on the prevalence of infidelity I have much enlarged, and intend soon to print; but I am chiefly employed on the continuation of 'History of the Christian Church'.

Northumberland, March 24, 1795, in which I have completed the sixty-second year of my age.

A short account of the last Illness of the Rev. Dr. Priestley, in a Letter from his Son Mr. Joseph Priestley, of Northumberland, in America, to the Rev. Theophilus Lindsey, in London

Though my father's general conduct in life, particularly on many trying occasions, sufficiently proved the value of his religious principles, and how much he was influenced by them, yet the force of them was so conspicuously displayed during his last illness and particularly the last three or four days of it, that for the benefit of myself and my children I have noted down some particulars respecting his behaviour at that time, hoping it may have the effect of encouraging myself and them in the cultivation of the same principles and the same pious dispositions.

Since his illness in Philadelphia, in the year 1801, he never enjoyed such good health as he had before done. Before that period and since the time he left England he scarcely knew what sickness was, and he frequently said he had never during any part of his life enjoyed such good health. He took great delight in his garden, and in viewing the little improvements going forward in and about the town. The rapidly increasing prosperity of the country, whether as it regarded its agriculture, manufactures and commerce, or the increasing taste for science and literature, were all of them to him the sources of the purest pleasure. For the last four years of his life he lived under an administration, the principles and practice of which he perfectly approved of, and with Mr. Jefferson, the head of that administration, he frequently corresponded, and they had for each other a mutual regard and esteem. He enjoyed the esteem of the wisest and best men in the country, particularly at Philadelphia where his religion and his politics did not prevent his being kindly and cheerfully received by great numbers of opposite opinions in both, who thus paid homage to his knowledge and virtue. At home he was beloved; and besides the advantages of an excellent library to which he was continually making additions, and of a laboratory that was amply provided with every thing necessary for an experimental chemist, he was perfectly free, as he had happily been through life, in consequence of my mother's ability and attention, from any attention to worldly concerns; considering himself, as he used to express himself, merely as a lodger, and had all his time to devote to his theological and philosophical pursuits. He had the satisfaction of witnessing the gradual spread of his religious opinions, and the fullest conviction that he should prevail over his opponents in chemistry. He looked forward with the greatest pleasure to future exertions in both these fields, and had within the last month or six weeks been projecting many improvements in his apparatus, which he meant to make use of upon the return of warm weather in the spring. Notwithstanding, therefore, the many trials he underwent in this country, he had still great sources of happiness left, unalloyed by any apprehension of any material defect in any of his senses, or of any abatement of the vigour of his mind. Consistent with the above was his declaration that excepting the want of the society of Mr. L., Mr. B. and two or three other particular friends, which however was made up to him, in some, though in a small degree by their regular correspondence, he had never upon the whole spent any part of his life more happily, nor, he believed, more usefully.

The first part of his illness, independent of his general weakness, the result of his illness in Philadelphia in 1801, was a constant indigestion, and a difficulty of swallowing meat or any kind of solid food unless previously reduced by mastication to a perfect pulp. This gradually increased upon him till he could swallow liquids but very slowly, and led him to suspect, which he did to the last, that there must be some stoppage in the aesophagus. Latterly he lived almost entirely upon tea, chocolate, soups, sago, custard puddings, and the like. During all this time of general and increasing debility, he was busily employed in printing his Church History, and the first volume of the Notes on Scripture; and in making new and original experiments. During this period, likewise, he wrote his pamphlet of Jesus and Socrates compared, and re-printed his Essay on Phlogiston. He would not suffer any one to do for him what he had been accustomed to do himself; nor did he alter his former mode of life in any respect, excepting that he no longer worked in his garden, and that he read more books of a miscellaneous nature than he had been used to do when he could work more in his laboratory, which had always served him as a relaxation from his other studies.

From about the beginning of November 1803, to the middle of January 1804, his complaint grew more serious. He was once incapable of swallowing any thing for near thirty hours; and there being some symptoms of inflammation at his stomach, blisters were applied, which afforded him relief; and by very great attention to his diet, riding out in a chair when the weather would permit, and living chiefly on the soft parts of oysters, he seemed if not gaining ground, at least not getting worse; and we had reason to hope that if he held out till spring as he was, the same attention to his diet with more exercise, which it was impossible for him to take on account of the cold weather, would restore him to health. He however, considered his life as very precarious, and used to tell the physician who attended him, that if he could but patch him up for six months longer he should be perfectly satisfied, as he should in that time be able to complete printing his works. The swelling of his feet, an alarming symptom of general debility, began about this time.

To give some idea of the exertions he made even at this time, it is only necessary for me to say, that besides his miscellaneous reading, which was at all times very great, he read through all the works quoted in his comparison of the different systems of the Grecian philosophers with christianity, composed that work, and transcribed the whole of it in less than three months. He took the precaution of copying one day in long hand, what he had composed the day before in short hand, that he might by that means leave the work complete as far as it went, should he not live to complete the whole. During this period he composed in a day his second reply to Dr. Linn.

About this time he ceased performing divine service, which he said he had never before known himself incapable of performing, notwithstanding he had been a preacher so many years. He likewise now suffered me to rake his fire, rub his feet with a flesh-brush, and occasionally help him to bed. In the mornings likewise he had his fire made for him, which he always used to do himself, and generally before any of the family was stirring.

In the last fortnight in January he was troubled with alarming fits of indigestion; his legs swelled nearly to his knees, and his weakness increased very much. I wrote for him, while he dictated, the concluding section of his New Comparison, and the Preface and Dedication. The finishing this work was a source of great satisfaction to him, as he considered it as a work of as much consequence as any he had ever undertaken. The first alarming symptom of approaching dissolution was his being unable to speak to me upon my entering his room on Tuesday morning the 31st of January. In his Diary I find he stated his situation as follows: 'Ill all day – Not able to speak for near three hours'. When he was able to speak he told me he had slept well, as he uniformly had done through the whole of his illness; so that he never would suffer me, though I frequently requested he would do it, to sleep in the same room with him; and that he felt as well as possible; that he got up and shaved himself, which he never omitted doing every morning till within two days of his death; that he went to his laboratory, and then found his weakness very great; that he got back with difficulty; that just afterward his grand daughter, a child of about six or seven years old, came to him to claim the fulfilment of a promise he had made her the evening before, to give her a fivepenny bit. He gave her the money, and was going to speak to her, but found himself unable. He informed me of this, speaking very slowly a word at a time; and added, that he had never felt more pleasantly in his whole life than he did during the time he was unable to speak. After he had taken his medicine, which was bark and laudanum, and drank a bason of strong mustard broth, he recovered surprisingly, and talked with cheerfulness to all who called upon him, but as though he was fully sensible that he had not long to live. He consented for the first time that I should sleep in the room with him.

On Wednesday, February 1, he writes, 'I was at times much better in the morning: capable of some business: continued better all day.' He spake this morning as strong as usual, and took in the course of the day a good deal of nourishment with pleasure. He said, that he felt a return of strength, and with it there was a duty to perform. He read a good deal in Newcome's Translation of the New Testament, and Steven's History of the War. In the afternoon he gave me some directions how to proceed with the printing his work in case he should die. He gave me directions to stop the printing of the second volume, and to begin upon the third, that he might see how it was begun, and that it might serve as a pattern to me to proceed by.

On Thursday the 2nd, he wrote thus for the last time in his Diary: 'Much worse: incapable of business: Mr. Kennedy came to receive instructions about printing in case of my death.' He sat up, however, a great part of the day, was cheerful, and gave Mr. Cooper and myself some directions, with the same composure as though he had only been about to leave home for a short time. Though it was fatiguing to him to talk, he read a good deal in the works above mentioned.

On Friday he was much better. He sat up a good part of the day reading Newcome; Dr. Disney's Translation of the Psalms; and some chapters in the Greek Testament, which was his daily practice. He corrected a proof-sheet of the Notes on Isaiah. When he went to bed he was not so well: he had an idea he should not live another day. At prayer-time he wished to have the children kneel by his side, saying, it gave him great pleasure to see the little things again, he gave them his blessing.

On Saturday, the 4th, my father got up for about an hour while his bed was made. He said he felt more comfortable in bed than up. He read a good deal in bed, and looked over the first sheet of the third volume of the Notes, that he might see how we were likely to go on with it; and having examined the Greek and Hebrew quotations, and finding them right, he said he was satisfied we should finish the work very well. In the course of the day, he expressed his gratitude in being permitted to die quietly in his family, without pain, with every convenience and comfort he could wish for. He dwelt upon the peculiarly happy situation in which it had pleased the Divine Being to place him in life; and the great advantage he had enjoyed in the acquaintance and friendship of some of the best and wisest men in the age in which he lived, and the satisfaction he derived from having led an useful as well as a happy life.

On Sunday he was much weaker, and only sat up in an armed chair while his bed was made. He desired me to read to him the eleventh chapter of John. I was going to read to the end of the chapter, but he stopped me at the 45th verse. He dwelt for some time on the advantage he had derived from reading the scriptures daily, and advised me to do the same; saying, that it would prove to me, as it had done to him, a source of the purest pleasure. He desired me to reach him a pamphlet which was at his bed's head, Simpson on the Duration of future Punishment. 'It will be a source of satisfaction to you to read that pamphlet,' he said, giving it to me. 'It contains my sentiments, and a belief in them will be a support to you in the most trying circumstances, as it has been to me. We shall all meet finally: we only require different degrees of discipline, suited to our different tempers, to prepare us for final happiness.' Upon Mr. —— coming into his room, he said, 'You see, Sir, I am still living.' Mr. —— observed, he would always live; 'Yes,' said he, 'I believe I shall, and we shall all meet again in another and a better world.' He said this with great animation, laying hold on Mr. ——'s hand in both his.

Before prayers he desired me to reach him three publications, about which he would give me some directions next morning. His weakness would not permit me to do it at that time.

At prayers he had all the children brought to his bed-side as before. After prayers they wished him a good night, and were leaving the room. He desired them to stay, spoke to them each separately. He told Joseph to treat his father and mother, when they should be old and sick, as they had treated him. He exhorted them all to continue to love each other. 'And you, little thing,' speaking to Eliza, 'remember the hymn you learned; "Birds in their little nest agree," &c. I am going to sleep as well as you: for death is only a good long sound sleep in the grave, and we shall meet again.' He congratulated us on the dispositions of our children; said it was a satisfaction to see them likely to turn out well; and continued for some time to express his confidence in a happy immortality, and in a future state, which would afford us ample field for the exertion of our faculties.

On Monday morning, the 6th of February, after having lain perfectly still till four o'clock in the morning, he called to me, but in a fainter tone than usual to give him some wine and tincture of bark. I asked him how he felt. He answered, he had no pain, but appeared fainting away gradually. About an hour after he asked me for some chicken broth, of which he took a tea cup full. His pulse was quick, weak, and fluttering: his breathing, though easy, short. About eight o'clock, he asked me to give him some egg and wine. After this he lay quite still till ten o'clock, when he desired me and Mr. Cooper to bring him the pamphlets* we had looked out the evening before. He then dictated as clearly and distinctly as he had ever done in his life the additions and alterations he wished to have made in each. Mr. Cooper took down the substance of what he said, which when he had done, I read to him. He said Mr. Cooper had put it in his own language; he wished it to be put in his. I then took a pen and ink to his bed-side. He then repeated over again, nearly word for word, what he had before said; and when I had done, I read it over to him. 'That is right; I have now done.' About half an hour after he desired, in a faint voice, that we would move him from the bed on which he lay to a cot, that he might lie with his lower limbs horizontal, and his head upright. He died in about ten minutes after we had moved him, but breathed his last so easy, that neither myself or my wife, who were both sitting close to him, perceived it at the time. He had put his hand to his face, which prevented our observing it.

THE END

* The pamphlets which Mr. Priestley here mentions were, The Comparison of Jesus and Socrates, and two pamphlets in defence of it.

NOTES TO MEMOIRS

Childhood and Youth. 'It was my misfortune to have the idea of darkness, and the ideas of malignant spirits and apparitions, very closely connected in my infancy', *Examination of Reid* (Works iii 50). Timothy says, 'At four years of age Joseph could repeat the Assembly's Catechism, without missing a word. When about six and a half, he would now and then ask me to kneel down with him while he prayed', 35 f. The frost of 1739 'began on Christmas-day. Some people were frozen to death in the streets and fields, and upon the Thames, where several ships were sunk by the driving of the ice', *Chron. Hist.*, 1747, ii 364.

His brother Joshua was still alive at Birstal in 1815, aged 80, with a wife aged 84, in a 'very neat dwelling, quite in the style of simple country life'. P. had provided for their permanent support; the wife said, 'she could never hear the name of that good man mentioned without being overcome' (Rutt i 6). Timothy says P. 'rarely spent an hour for any recreation. From eleven to about thirteen he had read most of Mr. Bunyan's works, and other authors on religion, besides the common Latin authors', 36.

Kirkby died 1754, 'dreadfully afflicted with the stone', Timothy 36. Dr. Caleb Ashworth, born in Lancashire 1709, studied under Doddridge, then succeeded him; died July 1775. Graham preached to the dissenting clergy at Leeds *Repentance the only condition of Final Acceptance*; asserted that 'the doctrine of atonement was not known, nor believed in the world till many hundred years after our Lord and his apostles had left it': see his *Memoirs* 83, 85. Thomas Walker had been minister at Cockermouth, then at Mill-hill, Leeds, where he died 1764; his nephew was Rev. George Walker, F.R.S.

Spira, perhaps a fabulous character, came from a book, *The Horrible End of Francis Spira.* William Coward, a rich eccentric merchant, died 1738, aged 90: *Gent. Mag.* viii 221; *Corr. of Doddridge* iii 232. Baxterian: the doctrine of Richard Baxter (Kippis, *Biog. Brit.* ii 22) 'strikes into a middle path, between Calvinism and Arminianism, endeavouring, in some degree, though, perhaps, not very consistently, to avoid the errors of each'.

Dr. Conder was appointed at the Mile End academy in 1754, where he filled the divinity-tutor's chair nearly 27 years, dying 1781. Ten Calvinist Articles: they insisted on the Resurrection for 'the same numerical bodies' ('numerical' dropped in 1805).

Doddridge died 1751, aged 49, at Lisbon. He was the last nonconformist teacher to be cited before the Spiritual Court (for presiding over the seminary at Northampton with episcopal license); but the judges 'ordered a prohibition to be issued', *Biog. Brit.* v 366; *Corr. of D.* iii 108, 139.

Daventry. Rutt i 22 says he was the 4th pupil on Belsham's list. For Clark, *Biog. Brit.* v 299 f. Doddridge's book was *A Course of Lectures on the principal subjects of Pneumatology, Ethics, and Divinity*, ed. by Clark, 1763; third ed. by Kippis, 1794. Collins wrote *Philosophical Inquiry Concerning Human Liberty*, 1715; reprinted by P. in 1790, Rutt ii 77 f. Alexander died at Birmingham, 1765: *A sermon on Ecclesiastes* ix 10, 1766. In this work he supports the view that there is no state of consciousness between death and the resurrection; *Biog. Brit.* ii 207.

Friends: Holland, minister at Prescot and Ormskirk; Belsham says he was the first student who 'entered under Dr. Ashworth'. Whitehead, settled at Box Lane, near Berkhamstead, Herts. Caleb Rotherham, son of a tutor at a Kendal academy; when his father died in 1754 he removed to Daventry, whence he was invited by his father's congregation. Radcliffe Scholefield settled at Whitehaven, then went to Birmingham where he was minister at the old meeting-house till his death 1903: *M. Mag.*, 1803. Thomas Taylor became assistant-tutor at D., then chaplain to Mrs. Abney at Stoke Newington and preacher at Carter Lane, London. Stammer: P. refers to it in *Lectures on Oratory* (xxxv), Works xxiii 480.

Needham Market. Salary: Doddridge, in 1723, removing to Kibworth, his first settled place, wrote, 'The salary cannot possibly amount to above £35 a-year; but I think I may board for about £10 a-year', *Corr.* i. 219.

Benson: scriptural critic, died 1762 aged 62, *Biog. Brit.* 203H, 206; Kippis, *Life of Lardner*, pp. xii f. Kippis died 1795 aged 70: *Prot. Diss. Mag.* iii 1–6. Smithson went to Harleston 1755, to Nottingham 1758, where he died of a consumption 1769, ordering all his MSS to be burnt. Tomkin's book, 1732; see *Works* of P. vii 236. Tomkin died 1755: Toulmin in *Memoirs of Neal* (prefaced to *Hist. of Puritans*, 1822). Caleb Fleming died 1779, aged 80: *Life of Lardner*, p. xcvi: in *A Survey of 'The Search after Souls'*, 1758, he maintained the spirit's immateriality and 'the doctrine of an immediate resurrection-body', 308.

Lardner and 'another person': the other was Dr. Harwood (*Works* xxi 243). Taylor's *Paraphrase*, 1745; P. wrote on it 1784, see *Works* iv 57; vii 464. Opened up *Theolog. Repository*, 1769 (*Works* vii 514), see ii 158, 287, 400; iii 86, 188 (*Works* vii 365–416). Willetts: *T.R.* ii 304, 458; he died 1779 aged 81. The Rev. W. Turner, who married his eldest daughter, said, 'He had great mechanical ingenuity; and had cultivated with much success several of the branches of natural philosophy, particularly magnetism and optics. He was probably one of the first who inspired with a taste for philosophical investigations the afterwards justly celebrated Dr Priestley', see J. Toulmin, *Memoirs of the Rev. Samuel Bourn*, 258–63. 'Delivered at an ordination': of Thomas and John Jervis 1779: *Works* xv 82. Scott ordained at Ipswich, 1737, after preaching at Lowestoft: wrote four papers in *T.R.* (i 70, 73, 219, 448); died 1774. See notes to Intro. I 20 for his *Job*, 2nd ed. 1773. Gill, prob. Rev. Jeremiah Gill, Gainsborough (T.R. i 431, iii 382). Wadsworth names were Field Sylvester. Haynes wrote to a friend at Nantwich, from Sheffield 12 Dec. 1757, 'I think I could move a young gentleman in Essex (*sic*), viz. Mr. Priestley, who is a man both of genius and learning, but is too far to come on trial, nor can you afford to pay him for his journey, nor will, at all adventures, give him an invitation on my opinion of him,' Rutt i 42.

Nantwich. Eddowes: Ralph Eddowes of Chester who went to Philadelphia, 1793, seems of the family. Flure: see *Works* iii 53. Brereton seems the 'very sensible clergyman, an excellent scholar, and a person of philosophical taste', *Works* xxii 338. Harwood in his translation of *Abaazit's Miscellanies*, 1774, avows himself Arian and wishes 'my ingenious friend' Dr. P. would show his fallacies; by 1784 he came nearer P., Rutt i 44 f.

Crofts: his design was not completed: *An unfinished Letter to W. Pitt, concerning the New Dictionary of the English Language, by Sir Henry Croft*; he wrote on Chatterton in *Love and Madness*; contributed the Life of Young to Johnson's *Lives*.

Warrington. Seddon was chiefly instrumental in founding the academy, stirring up principal merchants and others in Manchester, Liverpool, Birmingham and elsewhere: *Hist. Acc. of W. Acad.* cited Rutt i 46. See *Works of A. L. Barbauld* 1825 I xi 16–22. The academy ended 1783. Clark, in the *Hist. Acc.*, seems to join Orton in recommending Aikin, for whom, *Mem. of Wakefield* i 217–22. Taylor died 1761 aged 67. Seddon in 1758 letter to Benson thought P. 'besides his youth, and the disadvantage of a defective speech, as not yet of a reputation sufficiently established, though of very fair promise', and again stresses 'some hesitation and interruption in his manner of speaking', Rutt i 47.

Wife: Barbauld *Works* 39, 46; i 49 f. Mrs. Finch died 1803 a few months before her father; see his last letters to Lindsey. Anne her eldest child died 1809: Mrs. B's poem on her, Rutt i 49.

Canton (1718–72), clothweaver, who became master of an academy in Spital Square, 'in conversation calm, mild, and rather sparing than redundant', Kippis, *Biog. Brit.* iii 217 f., 22. Watson and electrical studies, *ib.* 216.

Percival, a native of Warrington, first student there 1757, died 1804 aged 64; his son wrote a *Memoir* to his Works, 4 vols.

Seddon of Manchester: preached there till death in 1769 aged 53; *Mem.* by R. Harrison in his *Sermons on the Person of Christ*. Vaughan: P. dedicated to him his *Treatise on Education*, *Works* xxv 3; he died at Hackney, 1802, aged 82. His sons: P. discusses in letters to Price the charge, says that it cannot be less than £50 a year: Rutt i 59 f. T. Potter became a Manchester merchant. John Mort died 1788, H. Toulmin wrote *A Short View of his Life and Character*, see also *Gent. Mag.*, Feb. 1788; Barbauld, *Works* i 49.

Getecre died of an apopleptic fit at Holland's house, 1807.

Enfield, tutor in Philosophy and Belles Lettres, also minister on death of Seddon, 1770: *Works* xxii 431; *Mem. of Wakefield*, 1804, i 223, 226, 385, 551, 557. The three men mentioned by P. got together in *Three Discourses* 1780.

Leeds. Ordained 18 May 1762. S. Parkes mentions P. 'walking to time, or pacing at a set step. He spoke a single word at every step, and, by constant repetition of these practices, acquired a habit of pacing', Rutt i 63.

Turner of Wakefield, died 1794 aged 79 a few months after P.'s emigration. See *Works* xxi 450 n. Plan of *Rep.*, *Works* vii 520 n. Fothergil, physician, died 1780: Letsome, *Memoirs of John Fothergill* 1786 63.

Trial of Elwall: *The Triumph of Truth, being an Account of the Trial of Mr. Elwall for Heresy and Blasphemy, at Stafford Assizes, 1726: Works* ii 417.

John Smeaton, engineer, died 1794 aged 68; constructed Eddystone Lighthouse and Ramsgate Harbour.

Newsome Cappe, died 24 Dec. 1800 near end of 67th year: *Memoir* by widow in his *Critical Remarks* 1802. He held view of uninterrupted consciousness at death.

Blackburne died 1787, in 83rd year: his *Works*, 1804, i 67; *Univ. Theol. Mag.*, 1805, iii, iv, indices. Belsham sets the visit in early summer 1769: *Mem. of Lindsey* i 34; *Works* v 3; xxi 450. His son Francis died 1816, vicar of Brignal near Greta Bridge; edited his father's *Works* in 7 vols.

Lindsey had been collated to Catterick, 1763, on death of Mrs. Cappe's father; he resigned the vicarage 1773; died 1808 aged 85. For leaving Catterick: *Memoirs of Mrs Cappe*, 1823, 165; Belsham, *Mem. Lindsey* 88. In London at Featherstone Buildings, Holborn, *Mem.* 91–8.

Lee became Solicitor-General 1782; died 1793 aged 60; P. *Works* iv 3, xxii 453, xxv 393–5.

Calne and Lord Shelburne. Timothy P. 28 says Lord S. 'while in Italy, had been rendered anxious for his acquaintance, from the high renown which the abilities and performances of Dr. P. had acquired for him abroad, while as yet he was but little known in his native land'.

Magellan, John Hyacinth De, descendent of the great navigator, was a Portuguese

Jesuit, used by rich and noble persons abroad to get scientific instruments in Britain; he himself at times improved their constructions; he belonged to almost 'all the philosophical clubs and meetings in London', and had early news of European discoveries: Rutt i 198.

Hammon: Dr. Turner. Lady Denny died in Ireland 1758: *Gent. Mag.*, lv 235. She made an ingenuous contrivance 'for the benefit of infants'. Rutt i 201.

Bishop of Waterford: Dr. Newcome, Archbishop of Armagh 1795, died 1800: *Works* xx 121.

Third son Henry born at Calne, went to America with elder brother and died 1795 just after P. had fixed him a farm and built him a house.

Mrs. Reyner, died at Clapham 1800 aged 86: *Works* vi 3; *Mem. Lindsey* 119–21, 156, 359. She disliked P.'s doctrine. 'No', she would exclaim, 'I shall continue the same conscious being after death as I am now.' Rutt i 209. Morgan, *Mem. of Price*, says 'Some of his evenings in each week he devoted to particular parties; but the party in which he always expressed himself most agreeably entertained, and which met at stated times at the London Coffee House, Ludgate Hill, consisted of Dr. Franklin, Mr. Canton, Dr. Kippis and other philosophical gentlemen.' P. joined this gathering. Morgan 48 f.

Pension: *Works* xix 360. Salte, a close friend of Alexander, *Biog. Brit.* ii 207; died 1817; Edward Jeffries died 1814 aged 88; Radcliffe died 1809; Reynolds died 1814 aged 86; Galton, *Works* xix 365; Simpson died 1812 aged 66, *Works* xvii 423; Heberden, *Works* xii 388; Tayleur died 1796 aged 83, see *Mon. Mag.* i 351; *Mem. Lindsey* 138; *Works* iv 313, viii 562; Parker died 1817, *Works* xix 418. In his last ten years P.'s sight had been much injured by his experiments with the burning lens, which he much used in summer, Rutt i 216.

Birmingham. W. Russell died 1818 aged 77, *Works* xi 3; Index. Blyth: Toulmin, *Mem. of Bourn* 275: he visited at fixed times all his congregation four times a year. In 1782 P.'s Hartley was burned by 'the licensers at Brussels', *M. Mag.* xxxiv 521; *Works* v 13. *Monthly Review:* Dr. Badcock (see Rutt ii 327). Horsley in *A Charge to the Clergy of the Archdeaconry of St. Albans* 1783; *Works* xviii 38, contrast iv 150 (1778); Howes in *Observations on Books, ancient and modern: Works* xviii 310. Alarm to friends: *Mem: Lindsey* 220–35. *Repository* closed 1788.

Sleep: his son says, 'My father was an early riser. He never slept more than six hours. He said he did not remember having lost a whole night's sleep but once, though when awake he had often to suffer much from pain and sickness, as well as from other circumstances of a very afflictive nature,' Rutt i 343.

London. Talks with Belsham: see *Mem. of Lindsey* 375 f.; Works xv 513–5. Clergyman of Birmingham 'who employed the pen of Mr. Burn', *Works* xix 434. Wakefield, *A Short Inquiry into the Expediency and Propriety of Public or Social Worship*, third ed. 1792; *Works* xx 303. He omitted the passages on Price in third ed.

Rutt ii 298 f. prints a statement by Joseph Priestley the son:

'I entertained hopes at one time that my father would have continued the narrative himself; and he was frequently requested to do so by me, and many of his friends, in the course of the year preceding his death.

'He was requested also, in imitation of *Courayer*, to add, at the close of the Memoirs, a summary of his religious opinions. This could have counteracted the suspicions entertained by some, that they had undergone a considerable change since his coming to America; and it was thought by his friends, that such a brief and simple statement of all that appeared to him essential to the Christian belief, and the Christian character, would attract the attention of many readers previously indisposed to religion altogether, from not understanding its real nature, and judging it only from the corrupt, adulterated, and complicated state in which it is professed in all countries called Christian.

'It was suggested to him also, that as his society through life had been singularly varied and extensive, and his opportunities of attaining a general knowledge of the world, and a particular knowledge of eminent political and literary characters, very great, it would contribute much to the instruction and amusement of those into whose hands the Memoirs should fall, if they were accompanied with anecdotes of the principal characters with whom he had been acquainted; for he had a fund of anecdote, which he was never backward to produce for the amusement of his friends, as occasions served for introducing it. But his relations were never sarcastic or ironical, or tended to disparage the characters of the persons spoken of, unless on subjects of manifest importance to the interests of society.

'He meant to have complied with the above suggestions, but being at that time very busily employed about his "Comparison", and thinking his Memoirs of little value compared with the works about which he was then engaged, he put off the completion of his narrative until his other works should be ready for the press. Unfortunately, this was too late. The work he had in mind was not completed until the 22nd of January, when he was very weak, and suffered greatly from his disorder, and he died on the 6th of February.'

Le Courayer had left France to escape persecution and lived in England from 1728 till his death in 1776 aged 95; about 1751 Lindsey met him in the family of the Duchess of Somerset. He was a Unitarian, drew up a *Déclaration de mes derniers sentimens sur les différens dogmes de la Religion,* which in 1767 he presented to Princess Amelia with a request for it to be kept secret during his life; she gave it to her chaplain, Dr. W. Bell, who published it in 1787; a translation was made the same year, with a biographical account.

An Account of further Discoveries in Air

LETTER I

TO SIR JOHN PRINGLE, BART. P.R.S.

DEAR SIR, *March* 15, 1775.
Having been pretty fortunate in the prosecution of my experiments on different kinds of air, since the publication of my treatise on that subject, I think it due to the attention with which you have from the first honoured them, to give you some account of what I have lately done. I know that every new discovery, in any branch of natural knowledge, gives you pleasure; and it is peculiarly flattering to me, that you consider some of those, which I have been happy enough to make, in a light of some importance. As I have materials enough for another separate publication, I shall not trouble the Society with a particular account of my observations; but if you think proper to communicate to them the following very general account, as a mark of my respect for the Society, as well as for yourself, you will add to the many obligations you have conferred upon me.

To the marine acid air, which I had discovered at the time of my former publication, I have now added three more; *viz.* the vitriolic, the nitrous, and the vegetable. The vitriolic acid air is produced by boiling in oil of vitriol any inflammable matter, or almost anything that contains *phlogiston*; as oil, camphor, spirit of wine, charcoal, and most of the metals. For though this acid seems to have no affinity with some of these substances when it is cold, it affects them considerably, and particularly takes *phlogiston* from them, when it is hot; and by means of the *phlogiston*, of which it deprives them, it is early made volatile, so as to assume the form of a transparent air, like that of the marine acid; being as readily imbibed by water, and as readily forming a white cloud upon the admission of alkaline air. But the affinities of the vitriolic acid air with various substances, and many of the phænomena attending it, are strikingly different from those of the marine acid air. I thought it a little singular, that the solution of iron, zinc, and tin, in a diluted vitriolic acid should yield inflammable air; and that when boiled in the same acid concentrated, they should chiefly yield acid air, which is not at all inflammable, and cannot be confined by water. This, however, is in fact the produce of the process; and the very same as when copper, silver, or quicksilver is boiled in the same acid. From gold, platina, or lead, I was not able to procure any air at all by this means.

The vegetable acid air is as easily procured from the concentrated vegetable acid, as the marine acid air is from spirit of salt; and, I think, in greater quantity. This air also is perfectly transparent, is instantly imbibed by water, and makes a white cloud upon the admission of alkaline air; though several of its properties are exceedingly different from those of the marine or vitriolic acid airs.

The nitrous acid I have exhibited in the form of air, though only, as it were, for a moment; since no fluid, that I am acquainted with, is capable of confining it. The more I consider the nitrous acid, the more wonderful and inexhaustible the subject appears. The kinds of air which it forms, according to its various combinations with *phlogiston*, are, I believe, more numerous than all the kinds that can be formed by the other acids. Many of the phænomena which have lately occurred to my observation relating to it are, to me, altogether inexplicable; though I perceive certain analogies among some of them. Upon this subject I shall have a pretty long chapter. But, to avoid being tedious at present, I shall only observe, that by boiling various hard substances containing *phlogiston*, and especially charcoal, in the nitrous acid, I get genuine nitrous air, the very same that I get from the solution of various metals in that acid. At the time of my last publication I had not a large burning lens; and as the focus of the mirror cannot be thrown upon any thing in the form of a powder, or that requires a solid support, my experiments with the solar rays were exceedingly incomplete. I have now procured one of twelve inches in diameter; and the use of it has more than answered my highest expectations. The manner in which I have used it, has been to throw the focus upon the several substances I wished to examine, either *in vacuo*, or when confined by quicksilver in vessels filled with that fluid, and standing with their mouths immersed in it. I presently found that different substances yield very different kinds of air by this treatment; and though the reasons, or analogies, of the different products, in many of the cases, be sufficiently obvious, and such as I had conjectured *a priori*, yet in other cases I am not a little puzzled and surprized. Various metals yield inflammable air by this process; several saline substances yield fixed air; many metallic *calces* yield the same, and some of them a *phlogisticated* common air; and some of the precipitates, in which the nitrous acid was employed, yield nitrous air, in one or other of its forms. But the most remarkable of all the kinds of air that I have produced by this process is, one that is five or six times better than common air, for the purpose of respiration, inflammation, and, I believe, every other use of common atmospherical air. As I think I have sufficiently proved, that the fitness of air for respiration depends upon its capacity to receive the *phlogiston* exhaled from the lungs, this species may not improperly be called, *dephlogisticated air*. This species of air I first produced from *mercurius calcinatus per se*, then from the red precipitate of mercury, and now from red lead. The two former of the substances yield it pure; but the red lead I have generally met with yields a greater proportion of fixed air along with it. Another quantity, however, gave this air and hardly anything else. On what this difference depends I cannot tell; but hope to be able to investigate. That this air is of that exalted nature, I first found by means of nitrous air, which I constantly apply as a test to the fitness of any kind of air for respiration, and which I believe to be a most accurate and infallible test for that purpose. Applying this test, I found, to my great surprise, that a quantity of this air required about five times as much nitrous air to saturate it, as common air requires. Common air is diminished about one-fifth, by a mixture of one-half nitrous air; but one quantity of this air was diminished one-half, and another two-thirds, by the addition of twice as much nitrous air; and three times the quantity, left it little more than it was at the first. A candle burned in this air with an amazing strength of flame; and a bit of red hot wood crackled and burned with a prodigious rapidity, exhibiting an appearance something like that of iron glowing with a white heat, and throwing out sparks in all directions. But to complete the proof of the superior quality of this air, I introduced a mouse into it; and in a quantity in which, had it been in common air, it would have died in about a quarter of an hour, it lived, at two different times, a whole hour, and was taken out quite vigorous; and the remaining air appeared to be still, by the test of nitrous air, as good as common air. This experiment I also repeated, and with nearly the same success, with another mouse, and another quantity of this air, the virtue of which had been impaired. Examining all the degrees of the calcination of lead, I found nothing but fixed air, or a little *phlogisticated* common air, till I came to *masticot*, which is a state that precedes the read lead. This gave air about twice as good as common air, and the litharge, which follows the red lead, gave fixed again. Roman vitriol and sedative salt yielded air which was, as nearly as possible, of the same degree of purity with common air. My conjectures concerning the cause of these appearances are as yet too crude to lay before the Society. My present ideas of the last mentioned facts are, that, together with other observations which I shall lay before the publick, they afford some foundation for supposing, that the nitrous acid is the basis of common air, and that nitre is formed by a decomposition of the atmosphere. But it is possible I may think otherwise to-morrow. It is happy, when with a fertility of invention sufficient to raise *hypotheses*, a person is not apt to acquire too great attachment to them. By this means they lead to the discovery of new facts, and from a sufficient number of these the true theory of nature will easily result.

I have made many other original experiments of a miscellaneous nature; but I shall not take up your time with the mention of them in this place. If this imperfect communication gives you, or the Society, any satisfaction, I shall be very happy, and shall be encouraged to prosecute these inquiries as much as my leisure from other pursuits will admit. I am, &c.

LETTER II

TO THE REV. DR. PRICE, F.R.S.

DEAR SIR,   *April 1, 1775.*

As you are pleased to interest yourself in my experiments, I hope it will give you some pleasure to be informed, that, I think, I never was more successful than I have been in the few days that I have been able to attend to these matters, since my return into the country. By the heat of the flame of a candle, and catching the air that arises in the manner described in fig. VIII. pl. 2. in my late Treatise, I get the pure air I discovered in London in great plenty, from a variety of cheap materials; not only from red lead, but many earthy substances moistened with spirit of nitre and dried, as chalk and quick-lime; which demonstrates that red lead, *mercurius calcinatus per se*, &c. extract the nitrous acid from the air; and that this acid is the most essential among the various ingredients which compose the atmosphere. From tobacco-pipe-clay, and some other things, moistened with spirit of nitre, I get fixed air; which seems to prove that this species of air (which is a kind of acid) is a modification of the nitrous acid, and in some measure accounts for the existence of so much fixed air in the atmosphere. I believe this experiment is the first instance of the proper generation of fixed air from other principles. What we have got of it hitherto has been by dislodging it from substances, that were supposed to contain it. Notwithstanding red lead yields so pure an air, paint made with it diminishes common air, and makes it noxious, as much as white paint; which seems to prove, that it is the oil, that yields the *phlogiston*, which injures the air to which it is exposed.

LETTER III

TO SIR JOHN PRINGLE, BART. P.R.S.

DEAR SIR,   *London, May 25, 1775.*
As I am desirous to present to the Royal Society a general review of my
later observations on air, without troubling them with a detail of my
experiments, I beg you would lay before them the following particulars,
in addition to those contained in the letter which I took the liberty to
write to you, dated March 15, and in the extract from that to Dr. Price,
dated April 1, 1775, submitting the whole to the disposal of the Society.

I have found, that the earths of all denominations, even the crystalline
and the talcky, which are thought to be insoluble in acids, yield a pure
dephlogisticated air, when treated in the manner mentioned in my former
letters; but that the calcareous earths, and some of the earths of metals,
as red lead and the flowers of zinc, yield it in the greatest plenty. Upon the
whole, I think, it may safely be concluded, that the purest air is that which
contains the least *phlogiston*: that air is impure (by which I mean that it is
unfit for respiration, and for the purpose of supporting flame) in proportion
as it contains more of that principle; and that there is a regular gradation
from *dephlogisticated air,* through common air, and *phlogisticated air,* down
to nitrous air; the last species of air containing the most, and the first-
mentioned the least *phlogiston* possible, the common basis of them all being
the nitrous acid; so that all these kinds of air differ chiefly in the quantity
of *phlogiston* they contain; though with respect to nitrous air, there seems
to be a farther difference in the mode of combination. By attending to the
quantity of *phlogiston* contained in the substances with which the spirit
of nitre is mixed, any of these kinds of air may be produced at pleasure,
and sometimes all the kinds will be produced in the different stages of the
same process. White wood-ashes yield an exceedingly pure air; but the
least bit of charcoal in the ashes depraves the air; and if there be much
charcoal in them, the whole produce will be strongly nitrous. The
phænomena of detonation (which has been a very puzzling appearance in
chemistry) admit of a very easy explication by the help of my late experiments. It is generally supposed, that in this case a sulphur is formed, by
the union of the nitrous acid and the *phlogiston* of the body with which it
is detonated; which sulphur is so inflammable, that it cannot exist a
moment without decomposition: and it has been thought, that in the
process of making the *clyssus* of nitre, the acid is intirely destroyed or

changed. But, in both these cases, I have no doubt, that the acid enters into the composition of some of the kinds of air which are generated upon those occasions. I once mixed a quantity of the ore of lead with spirit of nitre, and when it was dry, put it into a gun-barrel, filled up to the mouth with sand, in order to collect the air that heat would expel from it, in the usual manner. The production of air was very great and rapid; and when the heat became considerable, all the contents of the gun-barrel were exploded with great violence, and a loud report, demolishing the vessel which I had placed to receive the air. The next time, putting the same materials into a glass vessel, and disposing the apparatus in such a manner as that the explosion could not affect the collected air, I found it to be very strongly nitrous. Such, therefore, I conclude to be the produce of explosion of gun-powder, since charcoal with spirit of nitre yields this kind of air. In the detonation of nitre with substances that contain little *phlogiston,* the acid may form common air, or air much purer than that.

As I mean these letters to contain a general outline of what I have lately observed with respect to air, I shall add, that by the favour of that most intelligent and generous chemist Mr. Wolfe, I have lately procured some of that phosphoric spar, from which a new mineral acid, first discovered in Sweden, is procured. This acid, as well as the marine, vitriolic, and vegetable, I throw into the form of air, confined by quicksilver; and thus have an opportunity of examining its affinities with the greatest ease and certainty. I shall in this place only observe with respect to it, that this acid air decomposes nitre, but not near so rapidly as the marine acid air; and that the salt which is formed by its union with alkaline air is not sensibly soluble in water. I am, &c.

P.S. Upon second thoughts, I am not so well satisfied with my conjecture, hinted in the letter to Dr. Price, that fixed air may be a modification of the nitrous acid, though the experiment there mentioned seems to make it probable. But I lay no stress upon any opinions, farther than as they may lead to the discovery of new facts.

BIBLIOGRAPHY

For a full bibliography of Priestley's works see the list issued by the Library Association and also Dr. Schofield's *Scientific Autobiography*; for Boscovich and related matters, L. L. Whyte. I give here only a working list.

Abrahams, H. J., *Ambix* xii 1964 44–71.
Anon., *An Enquiry into the Human Appetites and Affections, showing how each arises from Association*, 1747, 1753 (in Parr, *Metaphysical Tracts of the 18th c.* 1837, attrib. to Gay by E. Taggart on Locke 1855).
Belsham, T., *Elements of Logic and Mental Philosophy*, 1802.
Belsham, W., *Essays, Moral and Philosophical*, 2 vols., 1799.
Bolton, H. C., *Scientific Corr. of J.P.*, 1892.
Bower, G. S., *Hartley and James Mill*, 1881.
Child, J. M., ed. and transl. of Boscovich, *A Theory of Natural Philosophy*, 1922.
Collins, A., *Enquiry Concerning Human Liberty*, 1790 ed.; first ed. 1715.
Cowherd, R. G., *The Politics of English Dissent*, 1956.
Crowther, J. G., *Scientists of the Industrial Revolution*, 1962.
Darwin, E., *Zoonomia, or the Laws of Organic Life*, 1794.
Davy, H., (1) *Fragmentary Remains*, ed. J. Davy 1855; (2) *Coll. Works* vii 1840.
Edelstein, S., *Chymia* i 1948 123–7.
Gay, *Dissertation on the Fundamental Problems of Virtue*, prefixed to E. Law's translation of King's *Essay on the Origin of Evil*, 1732.
Geikie, A., *J. Michell*, 1918.
Geffen, E. M., *Philadelphian Unitarianism*, 1961.
Gibbs, J., *Joseph Priestley*, 1962.
Gow, *The Unitarians*, 1928.
Guerlac, H., *J. of Hist. of Medicine & Allied Sciences* xii (1957 1–12 P.'s first papers on Gases and reception in France).
Hall, A. R., *The Scientific Revolution 1500–1800* (2nd ed.), 1962.
Hall, J., *A Hist. of the Town & Parish of Nantwich*, 1883.
Hartley, D., (1) *Conjecturae quaedam de Sensu, Motu, et Idearum Generatione* (in Parr); (2) *O'servations on Man, his Frame, Duty, and Expectations*, 2 vols., 1749; (3) in 3 vols., notes etc. by Pistorius, Life by his son, 1791 and 1801.
Hill, E., in Whyte 17–101.
Holt, A. D., *A Life of Joseph Priestley*, 1931.
Kippis, *Life of Lardner*.
McKie, D., *Antoine Lavoisier*, 1935.
McLaughlan, H., (1) *Letters of Theophilus Lindsey*, 1920; (2) *Warrington Academy*, 1943; (3) *English Education under the Test Acts*, 1931; (4) *The Religious Opinions of Milton, Locke and Newton*, 1941.
Markovic, Z., in Whyte 127–52.
Metzger, H., *Newton, Stahl, Boerhaave et la Doctrine Chimique*, 1930.
Muirhead, P., *Corresp. of the Late James Watt*, etc., 1846.
Partington, J. R., (1) *A History of Chemistry* iii, 1962, with refs.; (2) with D. McKie in *Annals of Science* ii, 3, 1938; and (3) iii 4 (1938).
Priestley, T., *A Funeral Sermon occasioned by the Death of the Late Rev. Joseph Priestley*, 1805.
Reed, H., *Chronica Botanica* xi 1949, 285–396 (Ingen Houz).
Randell, W. L., *Michael Faraday*, 1924.

Rutt, J. T. (1) first two vols. of *The Theological and Miscellaneous Works* (of J. P.), 1817–32; (2) the other 23 vols. referred to as *Works*
Schofield, R. E., (1) *A Scientific Autobiography of J. P.*, 1966; (2) *Archives internat. d'Hist. des Sciences* lxiv 1963, 277–86 (electrical work); (3) Intro. to J. P.'s *History of Electricity* (reprint of 3rd ed. 1775), 1966; (4) *J. of Hist. of Ideas* (oxidation and return of matter) xxv 1964, 285–94; (5) *Chymia* ix 1964, 71–6 (water); (6) *Annals of Science* xiii 1957, 148–63 (background); (7) *The Lunar Society of Birmingham*; (8) in Whyte, 168–72.
Smith, J. W. Ashley, *The Birth of Modern Education*, 1954.
Thorpe, T. E., *Joseph Priestley*, 1906.
Toulmin, J., *Memoirs of the Rev. Samuel Bourn.*
Toulmin, S. E., in Wiener and Noland, *Roots of Scientific Thought*, 1957, 481–96.
Turner, W., *The Warrington Academy* (ed. G. A. Carter), 1957.
Weld, C. R., *Hist. of Royal Society*, 1848.
Whyte, L. L., *Roger Joseph Boscovich*, 1961.
Willey, B., *The Eighteenth-Century Background*, ed. 1962.
Williams, G. A., *Artisans and Sans-Culottes*, 1968.
Williams, J., *Memoirs of the late Rev. Thomas Belsham*, 1833.
Williams, L. P. (1) in Whyte, 153–67; (2) in *Contemp. Physics*, Sept., 1960; (3) *M. Faraday*, 1965.
Wilson, G., *Life of the Hon. H. Cavendish*, 1851.
Wolf, A., *A Hist. of Scientific Technology and Philosophy in the 18th c.*, 2nd ed. 1952.

Index

Place names appearing in this index have been spelt following the style used in the original manuscript.

Lisle, 99–101
Locke, John, 14, 26, 33, 34, 39, 40, 41
Lunar Society, 25
Luneville, 109

MACLAURIN, COLIN, 12, 72
Madan, Spencer, 27
Manheim, 108
Mann, Mr., 93, 114; Works, *Dissertation on the Times of the Birth and Death of Christ*, 93q.
Marum, Martin van, 26, 52
Masticot, 149
Mayence, 107
Mayer, Robert, 57
Meadows, Mr., 78
Mettrie, Julien de la, 34; Works, *Man a Machine*, 34q.
Metz, 109
Michell, John, 46, 48, 49–50, 95–6
Mill, John Stuart, 41
Milton, John, 40
Mort, Mr., 91
Murphy, Arthur, 49

NAIRNE, MR., 23, 96
Nancy, 108
Necessarian, 74–5
Newton, Sir Isaac, 12, 14, 19, 23, 33, 34, 46, 125: his principles, 46–7; Works, *Principia*, 33q.
Nimeguen, 105–6

OSWALD, DR., 41, 113

PAINE, THOMAS, 37, 38, 41
Palmer, Mr., 120
Paris, 109, 111
Parker, Mr., 118–19
Pembroke, Lady, 49
Percival, Dr., 90
Petty, William, 2nd Earl of Shelburne, 22–4, 97–8, 106–8, 111–12, 114–19, 122
Phlogiston school, 20

Phlogiston, and theory of, 22, 44, 51, 55–9, 147–52; composition of, 56
Pine, R. E., 49
Potter, Mr., 91
Price, Dr. Richard, 17–18, 27, 80, 89–90, 93, 98, 114, 115, 121, 129–30, 132, 150–2
Priestley, Jonas, 11, 69
Priestley, Joseph: birth, 11; education, 11, 70; early scientific experiments, 12; enrolment at Daventry Academy, 12; becomes assistant minister at Needham, 14, 78; moves to and preaches at Nantwich, 14, 84–5; as tutor at Warrington Academy, 14; becomes minister at Warrington, 15, 87; his marriage to Mary Wilkinson, 16, 87; degree of Doctor of Laws conferred, 17, 90; embarks on scientific career, 17; elected Fellow of the Royal Society, 17; interest in connection of electricity and chemistry, 17–18; experiments in electricity, 18; minister at Leeds, 19, 92; becomes Socinian, 19, 93; studies chemistry, 20, 94; invited to accompany Captain Cook on second voyage to South Seas, 20, 96; awarded Copley Medal, 20; discovers photosynthesis, 20; commences work on gases, 20–2; accepts post as librarian to Earl of Shelburne, 22, 98–9; introduces his *principe oxygine*, 23; offence caused by publication of his *Disquisitions*, 24; illness of, 24, 133–9; moves to Birmingham, his increased interest in theology, 25; societies supporting his views on the French Revolution, 29; moves to Hackney, 30, 129–30; emigrates to America, 30; death of his wife, 30; turns to interest in botany, 31; death of, 32, 139; his attachment to Dr. David